The Tauris British Film Guides series has since ␢␢␢␢␢␢ in 2003 contributed to the revaluation of British cinem␢␢␢␢␢, deep into key British films from the past hundred year␢␢␢␢␢ the project forward, I.B.Tauris has now entered an ␢␢␢␢␢d innovative partnership with TCM (Turner Classic M␢␢␢ premier movie channel dedicated to keeping the classic␢ ␢live for fans old and new. With a striking new identity␢ ␢s will continue to provide what the *Guardian* has called ␢␢␢␢␢ resource of critical work on the UK's neglected film hi␢␢␢␢␢

The series will continue to draw on al␢ ␢ ␢res and all eras, building over time into a wide-ranging library of informed, in-depth film gu␢␢␢s, demonstrating the variety, creativity, humanity, poetry and my␢␢ic power of the best of British cinema in volumes designed to be a␢␢essible to film enthusiasts, scholars and students alike.

TC␢␢ is the definitive classic movie channel available on cable, satellite ␢␢d digital terrestrial TV <www.tcmonline.co.uk>

JEFFREY RICHARDS
General Editor

British Film Guides published and forthcoming:

A Night to Remember: the Definitive Titanic *Film* Jeffrey Richards
The Dam Busters John Ramsden
The 39 Steps Mark Glancy
Whisky Galore! and The Maggie Colin McArthur
The Charge of the Light Brigade Mark Connelly
Get Carter Steve Chibnall
Dracula Peter Hutchings
The Private Life of Henry VIII Greg Walker
My Beautiful Laundrette Christine Geraghty
Brighton Rock Steve Chibnall
A Hard Day's Night Stephen Glynn
if.... Paul Sutton
Black Narcissus Sarah Street
The Red Shoes Mark Connelly
Saturday Night and Sunday Morning Anthony Aldgate
A Clockwork Orange I.Q. Hunter
Four Weddings and a Funeral Andrew Spicer

if....

PAUL SUTTON

I.B. TAURIS

LONDON · NEW YORK

Published in 2005 by I.B.Tauris & Co Ltd
6 Salem Road, London W2 4BU
175 Fifth Avenue, New York NY 10010
www.ibtauris.com

In the United States of America and Canada distributed by Palgrave Macmillan
a division of St Martin's Press, 175 Fifth Avenue, New York NY 10010

ISBN 1 85043 672 X
EAN 978 1 85043 672 0

A full CIP record for this book is available from the British Library
A full CIP record for this book is available from the Library of Congress

Library of Congress catalog card: available

Set in Monotype Fournier and Univers Black by Ewan Smith, London
Printed and bound in Great Britain by MPG Books, Bodmin

Contents

Illustrations

Acknowledgements

Thank you to the cast and crew members I interviewed for this book, Malcolm McDowell, Jocelyn Herbert, Rupert Webster, Brian Pettifer, Graham Crowden. All other production quotes, unless stated, are taken from preparatory publicity material. The extracts from Lindsay Anderson's diaries and letters are taken from the working draft of my book, *Lindsay Anderson: The Diaries* (Methuen, 2004). Continuing thanks to Stirling University. The photographs are from the author's collection and from Brian Pettifer.

Film Credits

Production Company	Paramount/Memorial Enterprises Ltd
Producers	Lindsay Anderson, Michael Medwin
Director	Lindsay Anderson
Screenplay	David Sherwin
from the script 'Crusaders' by	David Sherwin, John Howlett
Director of Photography	Miroslav Ondricek
Cameraman	Chris Menges
Production Design	Jocelyn Herbert
Editing	David Gladwell, Lindsay Anderson
Music	Marc Wilkinson
Casting Director	Miriam Brickman
Assistant Director	John Stoneman
Assistants to the Director	Stephen Frears, Stuart Baird
Sound Recordist	Christian Wangler
Dubbing Editor	Alan Bell
Dubbing Mixer	Doug Turner
Camera Operator	Brian Harris
Camera Assistant	Michael Seresin
Assistant to the Producers	Neville Thompson
Production Manager	Gavrik Losey
Production Accountant	Brian Brockwell
Assistants to the Editors	Ian Rakoff, Michael Ellis
Interpreter	Jirina Tvarochova
Production Secretary	Zelda Brown
Wardrobe	Shura Cohen
Makeup	Betty Blattner
Continuity	Valerie Booth
Construction Manager	Jack Carter
Electrical Supervisor	Roy Larner
Transport	Jim Hughes
Electrical Contractors	Lee Electrics
Production Processing	Humphries Laboratories
Length	10,005 feet
Running time	111 minutes
UK Release	19 December 1968
US Release	9 March 1969

CAST

Crusaders

Malcolm McDowell	Mick Travis
David Wood	Johnny
Richard Warwick	Wallace
Christine Noonan	The Girl
Rupert Webster	Bobby Phillips

Whips

Robert Swann	Rowntree
Hugh Thomas	Denson
Michael Cadman	Fortinbras
Peter Sproule	Barnes

Staff

Peter Jeffrey	Headmaster
Anthony Nicholls	General Denson
Arthur Lowe	Mr Kemp
Mary MacLeod	Mrs Kemp
Mona Washbourne	Nurse
Geoffrey Chater	Chaplain
Ben Aris	John Thomas
Graham Crowden	History Master
Charles Lloyd Pack	Classics Master
John Garrie	Music Master
Tommy Godrey	School Porter

Seniors

Guy Ross	Stephans
Robin Askwith	Keating
Richard Everett	Pussy Graves
Philip Bagenal	Peanuts
Nicholas Page	Cox
Robert Yetzes	Fisher
David Griffin	Willens
Richard Tombleson	Baird

Juniors

Richard Davis	Machin
Brian Pettifer	Biles
Michael Newport	Brunning
Charles Sturridge	Markland
Sean Bury	Jute
Martin Beaumont	Hunter
Ellis Dale	Motorcycle Salesman

Introduction

if.... was the second feature film made by Lindsay Anderson. His first, *This Sporting Life*, about a rugby player's embittered relationship with his landlady, made a full six years earlier, was wrongly categorised as social realism. To film-goers and critics, Lindsay Anderson was an Angry Young Man, a teller of kitchen-sink tales about working-class misfits. After all, he was a director at the Royal Court Theatre which, in 1956, had launched the 'movement' with the first production of John Osborne's *Look Back in Anger*. That production (and the subsequent film adaptation) were directed by Anderson's friend, Tony Richardson. Earlier in 1956, Anderson had screened Richardson's first film, a short about a jazz club, *Momma Don't Allow*, as part of the first of six 'Free Cinema' programmes at the National Film Theatre. The programme director at the National Film Theatre was Karel Reisz, who co-directed *Momma Don't Allow*. Reisz's solo debut short, *We are the Lambeth Boys* (1958), was screened in the last Free Cinema programme. Reisz's debut feature, *Saturday Night and Sunday Morning* (1960), was produced by Tony Richardson and starred Rachel Roberts, who would play the landlady in *This Sporting Life*. The male lead in *Saturday Night and Sunday Morning* was Albert Finney, who had been introduced to the London stage, at the Royal Court Theatre, in the seminal production of *The Lily White Boys*, directed by Lindsay Anderson. Anderson also directed Finney in his West End debut in 1960 in the world première of *Billy Liar*. When Finney had to leave *Billy Liar* to take up pre-contracted work with Osborne and Richardson (to play the title role in Osborne's *Luther*), Anderson replaced him with Tom Courtenay, who later played Billy in the 1963 film of the play directed by John Schlesinger. As an actor, Schlesinger had taken Anderson's stage role in Kenneth Tynan's production of *Hamlet* in 1948 when Anderson left to make his first film. As a director, Schlesinger had made the kitchen-sink film *A Kind of Loving* (1962), starring Royal Court actor Alan Bates. Before making *Billy Liar*, Tom Courtenay had had a notable success in the lead role of Tony Richardson's film *The Loneliness of the Long Distance Runner*.

Between producing *Saturday Night and Sunday Morning* and directing *The Loneliness of the Long Distance Runner*, Richardson filmed an adaptation of Shelagh Delaney's play *A Taste of Honey* (1961). In 1966, Anderson made *The White Bus*, a forty-six-minute film adapted from a Delaney short story. *The White Bus* served as a sort of blue-print for *if.....*

But *if....* was not a film of social realism and Lindsay Anderson was never a social realist. He was an artist. He shared the Royal Court's leftist goals of breaking the middle-class middle-brow stranglehold on London theatre (the well-made play typified by the 'drawing-room' dramas of Terence Rattigan and Noel Coward), and he strived always to make 'socially relevant' films, but he was neither inspired by nor influenced by the Angry Young Men movement, which was not a movement at all – it was a journalistic tag. When he came to make *if....*, and Reisz had returned the script to him without comment, his old alliances and friendships had long cooled.

This Sporting Life's roots in the British New Wave movement are plain to see, but there's a lyricism, or poetry, in the film that owes much to the John Ford, Robert Flaherty and Humphrey Jennings films of the 1940s; and there's a symbolism and a surrealism (e.g. in the 'spider-splat' scene at the finale), and a passion too that is uniquely Anderson's. The film is true to its 'Free Cinema' aims but it is not an Angry Young Man film, nor a kitchen-sink film. It's a 'Lindsay Anderson Film'.

Unlike the Reisz, Richardson and Schlesinger films of the British New Wave, and unlike *This Sporting Life*, *if....* was not adapted from a theatrical or a literary source. It was written for the screen. In the six years between making *This Sporting Life* and *if....* Lindsay Anderson, disenchanted with commercial film-making methods in Britain, took inspiration from theatrical and film productions from Poland, Germany, Czechoslovakia and India. In those six years, he spent almost as much time out of the country as he did in it. Only by removing himself and his art from the inhibitions and prejudices of his own country, and by immersing himself in the work of 'foreign' men, was he able to make a film about Britain that succeeded critically and theatrically in the global markets, and whose world reputation continues to grow.

ONE
The Context

In 1935, at St Ronan's prep school in Kent, a twelve-year-old boy persuaded two fellow pupils to help him put together a magazine. The magazine, which ran for four issues, was called *St Ronan's News*. The boy was Lindsay Anderson. He wrote the film reviews. One of the reviews was of *Kid Millions*, an American film starring Eddie Cantor. In his review, Lindsay noted with approval that at the finale the film changed from black-and-white into colour and featured an assembly of orphans and a reformed gangster shooting cherries out of a machine-gun.[1]

From St Ronan's, Lindsay, the schoolboy, moved to Cheltenham College, and from Cheltenham, in 1942, to Oxford University where, for a year before active service in the Second World War, he studied classics. In his first year at Oxford (he returned after the war to take a degree in English) he wrote an 'Untitled Screenplay'[2] with the aim 'to combine a present day theme with an authentic picture of features of English life all too frequently misrepresented by the movies'. His screenplay starts at a public school. It features three boys, one of whom 'is passing through a stage of "materialist" cynicism' and who 'indulges in a mild flirtation' with a female character called 'The Girl'. Twenty-six years later, images from the Cantor film would fuse with elements from the 'Untitled Screenplay' to add to the personal slant in the rewrites of a script by David Sherwin called 'Crusaders'.

THE SOLDIER

The closer one looks into Lindsay Anderson's life, richly documented in his *Diaries*, one finds more moments of inspiration. Here's Lindsay in 1942 – a student at Oxford but training for war:

> 18 July 1942: On the whole I enjoyed camp, though that does not necessarily mean that I would wish to repeat the experience ... Memories

that stand out are the extraordinarily poor and tuneless singing of our platoon, poor Robin's deafness, the frightful rush to get tidy in the morning, the horror of hearing Reveille at 6.30 (is there any sound more unpleasant?), shaving in cold water and the command 'Prepare to Double!' The Y.M.C.A. car with its scarlet cakes, its large cups of sweet army tea and its charmer behind the counter was a real delight.

The night exercise was a pretty complete flop largely through the puerile leadership of the platoon. I distinguished myself chiefly by having a violent scuffle with my own section whom I mistook for an enemy patrol and vice versa, during which I fired a blank straight into Section Leader Taylor's face, tripped backwards over a hillock, was wrapped up in my W.P. cape, interrogated vainly and at last released. I also mistook Platoon H.Q. for another enemy patrol and dashed madly past them in a valiant effort to save the situation by Getting Through with the warning. The attack – very badly carried out – gave rise to an absurd but amusing argument, or rather verbal fight between Brown and Wilson in which Brown, who was almost certainly wrong, won the victory by virtue of his undoubted superiority of rank![3]

Academic studies intermixed with war games; a 'sweet army tea' car, and the firing of blanks into a section leader's face all feature famously in *if....* , and mark the point where the Crusaders start their 'revolution' against the absurdities of victories by 'superiority of rank'.

In 1944, Lindsay transferred from an infantry regiment to the Intelligence Corps and sailed to his home country of India. He was born in 1923 in Bangalore, south India, to a Scots father and a South African-born mother. He moved to England in 1926 when his parents separated. On board the military ship to India, Lindsay Anderson got into an argument with the captain over the merits of Rudyard Kipling. Kipling had written the poem 'If', about the making of the Man of Empire. The poem begins: 'If you can keep your head when all about you/ Are losing theirs and blaming it on you ... '. It ends with: 'Yours is the Earth and everything that's in it/ And – which is more – you'll be a Man, my son!'

3 December 1944: I arrived on deck before breakfast ... And 'If' was produced, and Kipling designated one of our three greatest poetic geniuses (third to Shakespeare and Tennyson). And I made my second mistake. I said I did not like Kipling and, inevitably, mentioned with disfavour his jingoistic imperialism. Lalkaka nodded sagely, smiling a little. 'I thought', he said, 'we'd come to that.' The upshot of it was

that I was invited to a Kipling session in the lounge after breakfast, so that the Captain might have an opportunity to enlighten me as to Kipling's true worth. The luckless Bernard who approached us on B Deck Square was also roped in.

After breakfast, there was Lal. in the lounge with his two volumes of Kipling before him on the card table. He began with the 'Ballad of East and West' – a silly piece of rubbish about the Colonel's son and the ever-so-sporting Indian brigand. This was read, not as a narrative poem, but as a weighty serious [poem] of profound philosophic truths. Now and then, as we came to a particularly odious line, Lalkaka would beam slightly and wink one of his black glistening eyes in a manner that made one want to shudder and scream.

The reading was exhausting. The continual strain of keeping up an expression of interest and surprise at this revelation of Kipling's greatness of mind, of continually smiling appreciatively at these nauseating sentiments and vulgar, blatant, superficial versification, and of murmuring from time to time 'yes, that's very good' or 'yes, I hadn't realised he was like that', seriously depleted my store of nervous energy, and after our merciful release (having to go to the Orderly Room) clasping one volume of Kipling each, I had to take two tablets of Aspirin.[4]

Returning to Oxford after the war, Lindsay's goal to make a film that combined 'a present day theme with an authentic picture of features of English life' was given an inspirational shot in the arm by his seeing the much-praised British war film, *The Way to the Stars*, written by Terence Rattigan and directed by Anthony Asquith, the ex-Prime Minister's son. The film, starring Trevor Howard, was said to be about 'life' on an RAF base during the war. Everyone in the film had a stiff upper lip and was thoroughly decent and utterly false. Here's a diary entry from Lindsay's life on a British military base during the real war:

27 November 1943: The [officers'] mess is as usual full of little parties gambling at poker, vingt-et-un etc. Is it mere prudishness, puritanism that makes me disapprove so? I think not. There is something, to my mind, repulsive about the atmosphere of such games. Something reminiscent of third-class railway carriages, stale cigarette smoke, 'virile' sex talk and beer slopping over the tables in Betty's Bar. A Canadian party was rather more obstreperous, because drunker, than the rest, and started singing. To anyone trying to write letters this was intolerable. I remonstrated but Tommy Braithwaite, drunk, merely said fuck off, adding that they didn't give a fuck who fucking well wanted to write

letters. In the white heat of anger I wrote a complaint on the suggestions book and resumed my seat – any more immediate action would have ended in a fight or ignominy, probably both. However, Sam Holloway read out the complaint to his table, causing great indignation and a cry of 'split-arse' from Jimmy Brown.

How wrong was I when I wrote deploring the philistinism of college? I have lately conceived a distaste for the senior public school types who too often lack the bluff (if stupid) good nature of the hearty, and substitute only a shallow, smart cynicism and a habit of talking as if all their verbs and nouns began with a capital letter. The education of character is not enough and even in my present mood I cannot deny that academically a Cheltenham education left a lot to be desired. Would I rather have been educated elsewhere? I doubt it. There was scope enough for individuality at Cheltenham.[5]

British army officers also liked to give themselves a thrill by bullying:

12 December 1943: Yesterday, the morning ended with a CO's drill parade: for this I had blanco'ed gaiters and sling and pressed my trousers. My web belt I had to leave because I was on guard the night before: I could have polished the brass but didn't because I was lazy and one not having to seemed sufficient excuse. But, of course, we weren't given time to change properly before the parade and on dismantling my equipment, I found the belt was far too loose; there was no time to alter it and I prayed for the best.

We were paraded on the asphalt outside the block; the sun shining fiercely in our eyes; the colonel, accompanied by a huddle of terser officers, began, slowly and methodically, to inspect us. I felt I was in for trouble.

When the colonel arrived before me his basilisk-eyes flew to my belt. He pulled at it distastefully. 'You must fit your belt properly – and it's in a disgusting state anyway.' I had aroused suspicion and was now subjected to minute examination. My cap badge was also disgusting (not black) 'and your boots are pretty filthy – altogether a pretty damn bad turn out'. The sun was glaring into my eyes as I gazed, with flickering eyelids, across the square. I felt myself blushing. I felt rather wretched. The colonel turned sternly to Sergeant Mace. 'Sergeant, see this cadet is chased, get his turn out smartened up' and with another mutter of 'appalling' or 'quite disgusting' he moved to the next unfortunate.

At first I was highly embarrassed, self-conscious and, as I say,

wretched: angry too with an impotent anger at the intolerable position one is in, against unkindness, insensibility, against the army. What
right has a man like that to humiliate me? (for I was humiliated). We
were marched onto the square and, as we drilled, anger gave place
to scorn: my ego reasserted itself, not that I could pretend not to be
affected by an incident like that, but I could see that it was largely
unimportant and that my offence and hurt was not to be worried over.
Throughout the parade I was checked by Sergeant Lewis. Evidently I
am a marked man.[6]

The 'whips' or the prefects of *if....*, are drawn at least in part from
Anderson's experience not only of public school life, but of British
military life – falsely presented in the Asquith film:

> 28 April 1946: I want to write something about British films – the time
> is ripe for constructive criticism. There is too much adulation flying
> about at the moment ... later this morning I went to see Michael [friend
> at Oxford] and unburdened to him my soul on the subject of *The Way
> to the Stars*, which we discussed – I becoming more and more vehe-
> ment in my condemnation as the nauseatingly smug sanctification of
> English inhibition and class prejudice appeared to me more and more
> distinctly in its true form.[7]

SEQUENCE

At Oxford, to champion film-makers he thought worth championing
– such as John Ford, Robert Flaherty and Luis Buñuel – and to pour
scorn on over-praised British films, Anderson founded a film magazine
called *Sequence*. His first issue, published in 1947, included a long essay,
'Angles of Approach':

> We may regard people who go the cinema of set purpose 'to be enter-
> tained' (or rather 'only to be entertained') as misguided, but there is not
> much we can say to them ... Better, really, that they should leave the
> cinema alone altogether than ... confess themselves too lazy to cope with
> *Ivan the Terrible* ... The lowbrow demands diversion, nothing more.
> The middlebrow, however, is on the high road to Art and Culture. He
> is aware, just, of what we may call fundamentals, and he thinks that a
> good film should show itself aware of them too. But he is incapacitated
> by a dislike of reality – reality plain, that is; what he likes, what he
> rapturously accepts, is reality romanticised. It is the prevalence of this

trait that is largely responsible for the present inflated reputation of the British cinema ... Mr Stonier writes in his *Vogue* article, 'The Coming Heyday of British Films' 'is not merely that they give a true picture of life, but that in doing so they rouse and satisfy. They represent, in fact, as syrupy fiction cannot, an attitude to living and to the art of the cinema, their drama is not pre-determined ... ' And this, if you please, of a list which includes *In Which We Serve*, most handsome of mock-heroic fakes, and *The Way to the Stars*. Has Mr Stonier ever analysed the plot of *The Way to the Stars*? If he does, he will find it the epitome of all the popular West End successes of the last ten years – young lovers, comic background characters, misunderstandings, happy ending and all ... I can, in fact, think of no two epithets that describe it better than 'syrupy' and 'pre-determined'.[8]

Sequence, which ran for fourteen issues, secured Anderson film writing jobs on the *Observer*, *The Times*, *Sight and Sound* and the *New Statesman*, the last of which he was sacked from in 1958 for refusing to join in the media praise of *The Bridge on the River Kwai*. He used his column instead to write about *A Generation* by Andrzej Wajda.

FREE CINEMA

In 1948, Lois Sutcliffe, a subscriber to *Sequence*, who ran the Wakefield Film Society, invited Anderson to make his first film – *Meet the Pioneers* – a documentary about innovations in the engineering firm owned by her husband. Between 1948 and 1954, Lindsay made four films for the Sutcliffes, films grounded in reality, filmed with real people doing real work in real places. The films were not merely instructional. When, at the start of 1954's *Trunk Conveyor*, the noise of heavy machinery fades to silence over rhythmic images of men and coal-faced boys at work, and on the soundtrack, in local dialect, a single man starts singing: 'I was born one day when the sun didn't shine, I picked up a shovel and I started to the mine. I loaded sixteen tons of number 9 coal and the keeper shouted God Bless My Soul!' the viewer knows that the film-maker is an artist. What one is seeing is film poetry of the kind pioneered by Flaherty and Jennings and Ford, a place and a mood and a people captured on film by a film-maker with a committed point of view. He sees and records not merely the men's work, but their humour too and their spirit, their nobility, their sadness. This would be the theme of two award-winning films Anderson made during the same period, the Oscar-winning *Thursday's Children* (1953), about a school in Margate for deaf and dumb infants; and *Every Day Except Christmas* (1957), a forty-minute film about Covent Garden porters, which won the Grand Prize for Documentary at the Venice Film Festival.

But Lindsay's award-winning films were not appreciated in Britain. His personal, poetic films were at odds with an industry and a public that lapped up middle-class mediocrity and stereotypes. Unable to generate interest in his films among those who controlled film distribution, bought films for television, wrote film journals and contributed to the national press, Anderson hired the National Film Theatre in London and, in six different programmes between 1956 and 1958, screened his own films and the early works of 'committed individuals' such as Tony Richardson, Karel Reisz, François Truffaut and Claude Chabrol. To drum up press interest he called this 'Free Cinema' and he issued a manifesto:

> These films were not made together; nor with the idea of showing them together. But when they came together, we felt they had an attitude in common. Implicit in this attitude is a belief in freedom, in the importance of people and in the significance of the everyday. As film-makers we believe that no film can be too personal. The image speaks. Sound amplifies and comments. Size is irrelevant. Perfection is not an aim. An attitude means a style. A style means an attitude.[9]

Under Lindsay Anderson's leadership, films were to become more intimate, less restricted, closer to life. In a letter to Allison Graham (8 June 1979), he wrote:

> There was no such thing really as the 'angry movement', there was a period of what we might call radical breakthrough, of which Free Cinema was a part. Yes, I do think that the breaking down of bourgeois restrictions of theme and style was an important achievement: certainly the Free Cinema films did enormously extend the range of experience tackled by British films. Working-class actors and writers – chiefly from the North – appeared for the first time, and in this respect *This Sporting Life* was characteristic of the period.[10]

In 1985, Anderson made a Thames television documentary called and about 'Free Cinema'. He outlined the programme's aims in a letter to Tony Richardson:

17 October 1985:
My dear Tony,
    I was very pleased when I was told that we could, after all, use

extracts from Woodfall Pictures [Richardson's British film company] – after I'd been assured by Thames TV that there was not possibility of getting hold of them. As if one could possibly do a programme about Free Cinema without showing your films!

I've thought of you very often while I've been working on this accursed programme – hearing so clearly your voice disapproving of the whole idea as a waste of time and probably destructive. I wouldn't argue with you. What happened was that Kevin Brownlow and David Gill, who'd done that marvellous 'Hollywood' series together, were commissioned by Thames to do a series about British Film Year ... a piece of 'prestige' (and essentially commercial) puffery, inspired by David Puttnam and Richard Attenborough ... Of course neither Kevin nor David Gill care tuppence about the British cinema, and who's to say they're wrong? So they formed an idea to get the programmes done for them by a handful of directors, making their own 'statements' or whatever on the subject ... I chose to do a programme about Free Cinema, largely because our work – with the exception of *Tom Jones*, because it won an Oscar – has gone completely without mention in the *British Film Year Catalogue of Achievement*. I know you'll shrug and say 'What's it matter?', and you're absolutely right of course. Yet there's an obstinate, if diminishing pugnacity in me that isn't quiet ready to lie down. After this experience, it probably will be.

I also know that neither you nor Karel will be particularly pleased to have your feature films talked about as 'Free Cinema'. For the sake of compactness – and to justify the programme at all – I've had to falsify, or at least to simplify, a good deal. But again, 'What's it matter?' I've comforted myself with the reflection that none of us will have to look at the programme when it's done!

And it has given me the opportunity to say some quite nasty things about both Puttnam and Attenborough. You see, I've not given up putting my head in a noose.

(And anyway, I have no hesitation in classifying *The Hotel New Hampshire* as a Free Cinema film. I hope that won't annoy you.)[11]

THE ROYAL COURT THEATRE

In 1957, two years after playing a madman in Richardson's West End production of *The Changeling*, and a year after Tony Richardson's production of John Osborne's *Look Back in Anger*, Lindsay Anderson joined Richardson's English Stage Company at the Royal Court Theatre. Up until this point, Anderson had made only short and mid-length films, including five twenty-five-minute episodes as a director-for-hire on the Richard Greene 'Robin Hood' television show. At the Royal Court he was given rein to open out into feature-length drama. He directed Robert Shaw and a then unknown Peter O'Toole in the London première of *The Long and the Short and the Tall* (1959), and Albert Finney in the world première of the Brechtian musical *The Lily White Boys* (1960). Perhaps more importantly, in reference to *if....*, he worked closely with John Arden on bringing *Serjeant Musgrave's Dance* to the stage. *Musgrave* is a fierce and richly poetic play inspired by a British military atrocity in Cyprus. The production was designed by Jocelyn Herbert, who would design *if.....* A major prop was a machine-gun:

JOCELYN HERBERT: After I read the play I did some drawings which I showed to John Arden. He seemed to think it was the right idea. Lindsay came along and tended always to say 'No' at first. He'd say: 'Well, I don't think that will do!' A good example, which is absolutely typical of him, is that in the play there is a Gatling gun. There were two carpenters in the workshop at the Court who were terribly nice, we had done a lot of plays together. I was talking with one of them about the gun and he said: 'Can I have a go at making it?' And he spent hours making this Gatling gun. I don't know anything about guns but I thought it was absolutely brilliant. He brought it on stage and we were looking at it when some people came in at the back. I suddenly heard Lindsay's voice saying: 'Good Lord! What on earth's that! Terrible!' And this poor man walked off. That was the cause of my first real row with Lindsay. We had a terrible row. I said: 'You never think about anybody!' And, of course, he used the gun because it was perfect. That was very typical of Lindsay. Whenever he saw something for the first time he'd be frightened it wasn't right.[12]

Anderson functioned best in collaboration. He needed willing and inspirational collaborators. At the Royal Court from 1957 until he departed in 1975 with the first ever successful production of Joe Orton's *What the Butler Saw*, Lindsay Anderson not only honed his skills as a director of actors, as a creator of feature-length dramatic and satirical and poetic productions, but he began to assemble the team with whom he would make *if.....* Albert Finney would provide the production company; Jocelyn Herbert would design the film. In 1964, he found his composer: Marc Wilkinson. Wilkinson wrote the music for Anderson's production of *Julius Caesar* (designed by Jocelyn Herbert).

Anthony Hopkins played Metellus Cimber (and would make his film debut in *The White Bus*); Ian Bannen, from *Musgrave*; played Brutus; Graham Crowden excelled as Casca. Four years later, Crowden would be hired to play the bicycle-riding, song-singing, essay-losing history master in *if....*

GRAHAM CROWDEN: Although rehearsal time was limited (there had been a change of cast – Ian Bannen took over from Nicol Williamson, who had some kind of disagreement with Lindsay), he took the conspirators who murder Caesar, and anyone else who wanted to come, to a small cinema in Soho to see some clips of the assassination of President Kennedy. Afterwards I walked with him to the Piccadilly tube to get to Hammersmith where we rehearsed. I couldn't see why we were watching Kennedy's assassination and I said so – rehearsal time being so limited.

'Well, Graham,' he said, 'it's an event that was as world-shaking as the murder of Julius Caesar. It could be an influence on your thought process. The shock of such an event. Don't you think?'

That's a small example of how he worked. Totally committed to the text and the players.[13]

Thus, in 1964, Lindsay Anderson was producing a play about a political assassination and linking a historical event with a more contemporary killing. The assassination on film of a school headmaster and his school system was no doubt far from Lindsay Anderson's mind at this point but, as a young man, he had been excited by the thought of a plot to get rid of the headmaster at Cheltenham College; strangely enough, this came on the very day he saw a West End play about a troubled schoolboy, the day, in fact, on which he first saw the actress who would play the matron in *if....*:

5 March 1946: Tea with Peter Currie and Curtis and the Cheltonian Society Committee. Afterwards get onto the subject of Coll. and stumble on the track of a rather exciting anti-headmaster conspiracy, but unfortunately not operating from the humane but the reactionary standpoint. Must go over and find out more about this. Curtis was very secretive, but let quite enough out of the bag to be going on with. He is a rather unfortunate type, who had a most awful time during the war but can't keep it out of his conversation ('I've been beaten up several times by Japanese guards, and I can tell you it isn't pretty').

Saw Terence Rattigan's new play tonight, *The Winslow Boy*, elder son Dickie is reprimanded for his failure in Mods, and his addiction to ragtime, while poor Ronnie stands outside in the rain, frightened to face his father, a man whose tongue is ironic as his heart is golden. The boy, it appears, has been unjustly accused of theft and dismissed. Usual competent West End comedy drama type, expert, entertaining and unoriginal ... A lovely little sketch by Mona Washbourne.[14]

The year after his production of *Julius Caesar*, Lindsay Anderson played the deputy headmaster in a Royal Court production of a play set in a school. The play was 'Miniatures' by David Cregan. Nicol Williamson had the lead role of a kleptomaniac teacher. Also in the production were Graham Crowden, as a schoolmaster, and Mary MacLeod, as the school secretary. MacLeod would play the housemaster's wife in *if....*, walking naked through the corridors when the boys are away on their game of War.

MARY MACLEOD: When we were rehearsing, I felt very nervous because I hadn't been on stage for so long, and here I was surrounded by all these important people in the theatre [the cast also included George Devine and *if....* casting director, Miriam Brickman]. Also nobody laughed, and it was supposed to be a funny part. Suddenly I heard this dry little chuckle. It was Lindsay. He said he'd noticed that I'd done the part in three different ways, and told me which he liked best.[15]

CANNES, PESARO, INDIA, CZECHOSLOVAKIA, POLAND

Anderson's theatre work at the Court was not the reason for the six-year gap between making *This Sporting Life* and *if....* He'd had a hard time on set when he fell behind schedule early in the shoot and always struggled to catch up. After ten days there was serious talk of sacking him. Part of the problem was his relationship with Richard Harris, the film's star:

23 April 1962: The mixture of tenderness and sympathy with violence and even cruelty is astonishing, painful and of course endlessly fascinating. The familiar combination, I suppose of pride and insecurity, of sensibility and egoism: the inescapable formula for a star. All my reason tells me that this is a fatal temperament for me to become in any way involved with. Yet I am completely helpless. This mixture of power and sensitivity, of virility and immaturity, of insinuating charm and aggressive domination – how can I be expected to resist? Whether

1. *Filming the chapel scene with boys from Cheltenham College*

he [Harris] is embracing me physically, like some big warm dog, or ordering me to 'heel' – I am at his service completely.[16]

From 1962, for the next three years, Anderson wanted to work only with Richard Harris. They drew up an ambitious plan of films and plays. In 1963, Lindsay Anderson directed Richard Harris at the Royal Court in their own adaptation of Gogol's *Diary of a Madman*. It was to be followed with Harris playing Heathcliffe in Anderson's film of *Wuthering Heights* (scripted by David Storey; financed by United Artists); by *Julius Caesar* (Harris quit two weeks into rehearsals) and by a play and a film about Dylan Thomas, the hard-drinking Welsh poet. Ironically, the plans were scuppered by the success of *This Sporting Life*, which won Harris the acting prize at Cannes and an Oscar nomination. Hollywood and the world film community made offers that Harris's ego, pocket and career couldn't refuse. After three years of following Harris on to other men's film sets from Ravenna (Antonioni's *The Red Desert*) to Mexico (Peckinpah's *Major Dundee*), and tired of Harris's mood swings and stonewalling, Anderson dropped the Harris projects and sought inspiration elsewhere.

As a child, his passion for film was built by the products of Hollywood's Golden Age, films starring Greta Garbo, Bette Davis and Mary Astor. As a young man at Oxford, his film enthusiasm was still fixed on American product, in particular the films of John Ford, but he was keenly cultivating an interest in world cinema. At Oxford he had organised a Czech film festival. Importantly, he was a devotee of the new international film festival at Cannes, for which he wrote annual reports for *Sequence* and *Sight and Sound*. At Cannes he befriended pioneering film writers and film-makers from around the world. In 1987 he wrote:

> I was young in the cinema when I first came to Cannes. Cannes was young too – two years old. If you have only known the Festival in its years of maturity, you will find it hard to imagine the excitement, the vivacity, the sheer enjoyment of those youthful years. In the dreary fifties, Cannes was like a party at which we greeted every year our friends and fellow enthusiasts. Every year we competed for food and drink at the Casino receptions; every year we would run to the Croisette as the stars passed by in triumph. Remember the starlets on the beach? Remember Robert Mitchum on the Carlton Terrace, defying Cold War etiquette by shaking hands with a star from Moscow ('Don't do it, Bob!' shouted a cautious Preston Sturges).
>
> There was Cocteau, most courteous, most perceptive and most principled of all Jury presidents. There were cinephiles from all over the world: the young rebels from *Cahiers du Cinema*. My dear friend Gene Moskowitz, the legendary Mosk of Variety ... The return of Buñuel; the astonishing debut of Satyajit Ray; Wajda affirming himself and the Polish cinema with *A Generation* and *Kanal* ...[17]

In 1960, Gene Moskowitz distinguished himself by shouting down the boos of the festival audience at the screening of Antonioni's masterpiece, *L'Avventura*. That day thirty-five film-makers and critics banded together to write and sign a defence of the film. An international community of film-makers was emerging from within continental Europe, and it was this community, and the spirit it engendered, that inspired Lindsay Anderson to make *if.....* In 1965, after the festival at Cannes, a group of rigorously individual, or 'New Wave', film-makers held a conference at Pesaro. It was launched by Pier Paolo Pasolini, who delivered the first lecture,[18] and it took the theme of 'Criticism and the New Cinema'. Lindsay Anderson was one of the speakers (he talked about his sacking from the *New Statesman*), as were his friends from the

Polish and the Czech New Waves. He left the conference inspired, keen to make a work of film art to stand with the work of the new greats.

He spent much of the year travelling the world, including several visits to Poland and Czechoslovakia to see at first hand his international colleagues at work. This 'world tour' actually started before Cannes and the conference in January. Weary from the soul-sapping chasing of Richard Harris, Anderson had taken up an invitation to serve with Andrzej Wajda on Satyajit Ray's jury at India's first competitive international film festival. Here, in Delhi and Bombay and Madras, he saw dozens of films from Eastern film-makers – untouched by Anglo-Hollywood gloss and triviality – including several by Sri Lanka's Lester James Piries, with whom he became a lifelong friend. He spent a day with Sukhdev sighting shots for Sukhdev's new feature film. He attended retrospectives of Indian screen greats, such as Vankudre Shantaram. He travelled cross country to see forgotten films by promising students (not always profitably), and he spent a lot of time watching Satyajit Ray's work and talking about film:

27 January 1965: Morning tour with Satyajit Ray; the image and religious decoration-makers' quarter: then two superb decaying nabob mansions: classical displays of marble and columns and statuary: heavy mahogany and teak: art nouveau decoration: formal gardens running wild ... Stimulated to ideas of thriller set in Calcutta with these marvellous backgrounds.[19]

29 January 1965: Satyajit contacts about 3.45 turns up at 4.25: magnificently airy: I see how it should be done ... Go to studio, see a little boring studio shooting and chat to Ashok Kumar and director who made the Bengali *Wuthering Heights* ... Then we see Satyajit's *Ghost Story* from Tagore Trilogy, and four reels cut from his new film. *The Ghost Story* beautifully set and lit. I am envious.[20]

The visit to India gave him the desire to make a film there. He chose an Indian theme for the first film of his aborted two-picture deal with Orion in 1979 – *Empire*, a tale of an Indian Mutiny co-written with Ted Tally, who would win an Oscar for *Silence of the Lambs* – but for now, the pull of wanting to work with Richard Harris was too strong. He spent mid-February 1965 looking for locations for the Anderson/Harris film of *Wuthering Heights*. On the flight back from India, Lindsay Anderson stopped off in Prague. The Czechs were making feature films that seemed to have been built on the principles of his own 'Free Cinema'; truthfully human and delicately poetic films by Milos Forman, Jaromil Jires, Ivan Passer, Evald Schorm, Jan Nemec, Jan Kadar, Jiri Menzel, Vera Chytilova and others. Chytilova's *Daisies* would be given a London release in 1967 on a double bill with Lindsay Anderson's *The White Bus*. Anderson was met at the airport by Jaromil Jires, and shown Evald Schorm's latest film *Každy den odvahu* (*Courage Every Day*), a poetic-realist account of a young man's rebellion against the establishment. Lindsay noted in his diary: 'A fine and sober picture ... movingly honest. What lovely lighting!'.[21] He was so impressed with the film that he agreed to write the English subtitles and push for its release in Britain – then alone in Western Europe for rejecting Czech films for distribution. In Prague, he met other Czech film-makers, and promised to return as soon as he could. In late March, he stayed in Prague for two weeks, watching films, visiting studios, meeting all the main players and having a moment of genuine epiphany:

> 8 April 1965: Make for Zrouch [about forty miles from Prague] where [Milos] Forman is on location for his new film. Rackety car and bad roads, but plentiful chat and a refreshing stop at Kvyna Hera to inspect the simple and beautiful Gothic Abbey. Arrive [at] Zrouch, at the Bata shoe factory, about 12.30 just as the unit breaks after morning shooting. The usual situation doesn't faze me – only one more shot to make this afternoon: but Forman, a dark, genial and handsome young man, is very pleasant and welcoming and speaks good French. His cameraman, [Miroslav] Ondricek, is the nice-looking young chap I've seen in the Film Club: and a fine cameraman. I'm very envious – seriously, and consider the problem of trying to invite him, or all of them, to London. Forman remarkably welcoming: one feels immediately accepted, to watch shooting, rushes etc. Atmosphere, with two writers in attendance, marvellously relaxed and collaborative. Play billiards with Forman.

> 13 April 1965: To Barrandorf (Studios) to see the cut of Forman's film *Loves of a Blonde*. Full of superb and delicate poetic things: the reminiscence of Free Cinema is extraordinary: the drinkers, the National Anthem – but with of course a great 'something more'.

> 14 April 1965: Certainly when Jaromil pointed out today in the club that Britain was represented at Cannes this year by films directed by a Pole and an American [Richard Lester's *The Knack* and Polanski's *Repulsion*] – I felt that I'd been fooling about in a ridiculous way ... I would like to feel that this is a turning point – while at the same time

knowing that I remain so dependent on ambiance, on mutual support or atmosphere. And that won't change. Finished work on the titles [of *Courage Every Day*]. Spent evening at the club, with Forman.[22]

The dependence on 'ambiance, on mutual support or atmosphere. And that won't change' was a reference to the hard time he had on the set of *This Sporting Life*. The crew were not interested in sitting in on rushes and creating a work of 'art'; to him they seemed interested only in the money they were being paid and in the hours they were obliged to spend earning it. The attitude of the professional British crew, and the crews he had used to make television commercials, had played a major part in Anderson's reluctance to make more films. His vision at Zrouch, with Forman working in close collaboration with a technical crew all keenly working for 'him', with two writers in attendance should he feel the need to call on them was, he believed, the secret to the success of the Czech New Wave. It was the blueprint for how Lindsay Anderson would make films.

LINDSAY ANDERSON: I liked the whole way they were approaching the subject, not just the subject itself, but their whole method of working together. It reminded me of the kind of atmosphere we used to have years ago, when we (myself and Karel Reisz, Walter Lassally, John Fletcher) were working together on the Free Cinema films, and which it's practically impossible to get when you're making a full-scale feature film in this country. I suddenly asked Mirek [Miroslav Ondricek] a few days later, if he would come to England and shoot a film if there was any chance.[23]

Miroslav Ondricek, who had photographed Milos Forman's first film *Konkurs* and Jan Nemec's *Diamonds of the Night* and *Martyrs of Love*, and who would photograph Ivan Passer's *Intimate Lighting*, Forman's *The Fireman's Ball*, and win Oscar nominations for Forman's *Ragtime* and *Amadeus*, would photograph Anderson's *if....* and *O Lucky Man!*.

On 19 May 1965, *The Times* newspaper published a large article written by Lindsay Anderson: 'Nothing Illusory about the Young Prague Film-Makers'.[24] It began by attacking the 'trend-setters of the British Film Institute' who 'remain lapped in their dreams of Antonioni, Godard and Roger Corman': 'It is our fault if, in spite of an outstanding harvest of international awards ... hardly a single Czech picture has won commercial release here in the past three years.' In the article, he stressed:

2. *Michael Medwin, Miroslav Ondricek and Lindsay Anderson on the first day of filming.*

It was significant, and surely healthy, that the first two pictures I was shown both mirrored, without equivocation, the failures, distortions and crimes of the Stalin years. Nor were these the work of dissident youth [an important point to make for a film-maker in his forty-second year]. *The Golden Rennet* (symbol of aspirations betrayed) is directed by Otakar Vavra, who was making pictures before the war. The poetic summation of its sad hero, confronted in his fifties with the evasions and pretences of a lifetime, is done with a style and an ambiguity far removed from socialist-realism.

In the article, he wrote admiringly of ten films altogether, including Jan Kadar and Elmar Klos's *The Accused* and *A Shop on the Square* (for which he also wrote the English subtitles); Jaromil Jires's *The Cry* and Milos Forman's debut feature *Peter and Pavla*: 'This story of an affable, round-faced, puzzled, mildly misunderstood teenager has all the essential qualities. The tone is subjective, the story incidental rather than dramatic, the sensibility very fresh, very personal. The actors are rarely professional, but they perform beautifully. And the camera style has a continual, graphic elegance, neither "composed" in the old way, nor sloppy in the (sometimes) new.'

Reading the article today, it is clear that in analysing the films of the Czech New Wave, he was writing about the film he himself would make next.

In March, Tadeusz Lomnicki, the star of Wajda's *A Generation*, the film which started the Polish New Wave, and the subject of the article that prompted Anderson's sacking from the *New Statesman*, came to London to propose that Lindsay Anderson direct him, in Polish, in a production of *Hamlet* in Warsaw. Anderson agreed, and spent much of 1965 and 1966 flying back and forth from London to Warsaw (almost always via Prague) to work with the inspirational Lomnicki on the theatre project as it changed from *Hamlet* to John Osborne's *Inadmissible Evidence* (designed by Jocelyn Herbert). The second meeting with Tadeusz, and the men of the Czech New Wave, was in May 1965 at the Cannes Film Festival, followed immediately by the conference of film-makers at Pesaro. Lindsay emerged a man inspired:

> 5 June 1965: The return has to be faced. Alas I don't want to ... The last two weeks have reawakened my interest in the cinema – given me a context, if you like – but return to London brings those rapid sensations of negativism, fatigue, irony, being against and knowing oneself in an out-of-step minority. It is infinitely disagreeable ... To Karel [Reisz] and Betsy [Blair]'s about tea time. Karel incidently pouring cold water on both *The Mayor of Casterbridge* [with Robert Shaw] and the Warsaw *Hamlet*. I feel it's all wearing thin: I am nearer the Czechs! M & Mme Kadar drop in for a drink.[25]

The growth of his friendship with the Czechs, and his admiration for the film-making processes in Czechoslovakia, coincided with a strain in his friendships with film-makers in London, but before Cannes, Lindsay had committed to a film project put together by the Royal Court manager, Oscar Lewenstein: a three-part film from stories by Shelagh Delaney, to be made by Reisz, Richardson and Anderson. Anderson had chosen *The White Bus*, a story about a woman who leaves her London typist job, travels to her home town in the North, and joins the mayor and a party of foreign dignitaries on a bus trip round the town's social, cultural, educational and industrial facilities. The film became a blueprint for the epic comic satires of *if....*, *O Lucky Man!* and *Britannia Hospital*, a recognisable reality which dips into fantasy and has scenes that change from black-and-white into colour. The mayor was played by Arthur Lowe, from the cast of *This Sporting Life*, and soon to be the housemaster of College House in *if*.... In a scene filmed inside the public library at Salford, Lowe as the mayor reads the creed printed on the walls of the central dome: 'Wisdom is the principal thing: therefore get wisdom: and with thy getting get understanding.' The creed was used on a title card as the preface to *if*....

The filming of *The White Bus* started in the autumn, after an abortive summer in New York trying to persuade his childhood idol Bette Davis to appear on Broadway in Athol Fugard's new play *People are Living There*. Miroslav Ondricek was brought over from Czechoslovakia and immediately proved his worth:

> 16 October 1965: A fraught and hectic week, impossible to chronicle day by day or hour by hour. Mirek shines through and over it, with his ardent, warm, sensitive, humorous, vigorous, professional personality. He has an extraordinary capacity to move from the boyish to the calmly authoritative with no effect or self-consciousness. It is a triumphant vindication of intuition ... From the first, I can't think of a moment when his attitude has not been what I would call correct – i.e. 'perfect'! He came through that door at London Airport – a bit pale, bit excited – and courageous too after all (for he didn't know me at all): and it was straight to work – discussing film stocks and lenses and cameras – yet equally such a sensitive, humorous, artist's response to everything he sees and experiences – 'Fantastish!' ... Mirek has a kind of response that I crave – sympathetic, dynamic, one that puts the project first, with the authority of a genuine sensibility – something God-given. And what a clean, sensitive, healthy fellow.[26]

With a key figure of the Czech New Wave at his side, Lindsay was back in the business of making films. *The White Bus* premièred in Czechoslovakia in February 1966.

In August and early September 1966, Anderson served on the jury at the Venice Film Festival, immersed again in the world culture of film. He was most taken by two very contrasting films: the poetic-realism of Gillo Pontecorvo's *The Battle of Algiers*, a tale of the French army wiping out freedom fighters bombing for Algerian independence, and the hallucinatory *Chappaqua*, from a surrealistic autobiographical poem by Conrad Rooks (the tale of a junkie told within a vision of ancient peyote ceremonies, with pop song asides). It's unlikely that these films had any direct influence on the fantasy-tinged realism of *if*...., and of *O Lucky Man!*, which followed, but all was adding to Anderson's knowledge of film craft: new styles, new approaches.

The last three months of the year were spent in Poland, renewing friendships with Wajda and the leading figures of the Polish New Wave, and completing work on the Lomnicki/Anderson production of *Inadmissible Evidence*, which opened at the Contemporary Theatre in Warsaw in December 1966. Before his trip out to Poland, he had assembled a film production team – set designer, composer, cinematographer – with whom he was keen to work; and with Crowden, MacLeod and Lowe he had the makings of a fine cast. But until late 1966, after the elimination of the Richard Harris projects, he lacked a suitable subject. He turned down several offers from Robert Shaw, including directing him in an adaptation of *The Mayor of Casterbridge*; and was almost tempted into film work by a script about the Marquis De Sade. In boyhood Lindsay Anderson had noted the sexual attraction of fantasy violence:

> 19 April 1947: The new Alan Ladd film, *Wild Harvest*, is about to appear in the West End. The advertisement consists of a clenched fist round which is wound a leather belt, the buckle outwards just waiting it seems to make contact with someone's jaw – or even, with its sharp point, to put out someone's eye. Round the wrist of this fist is hung a chain with an identification bracelet on it. It is hard enough to control my masochistic imagination as it is without having this sort of thing thrust at me in my daily paper – even to write about it gives me a rise. How many people are similarly affected? Women, of course, are proverbially fond of being dominated – is it merely an appeal to that, no more? Where does one draw the line between that and masochism? Presumably the answer is that our emotions have become coarsened, crude; now all sensations have to be violent to be felt at all.[27]

But his close friend, Jill Bennett, turned down the de Sade project and his desire to make the film vanished. In 1967, he very nearly agreed to direct *All Neat in Black Stockings* with a crew assembled by his old friend, Leon Clore, but he scotched the idea after working with Clore's crew on a Kellogg's commercial:

> 31 May 1967: Leon at rushes plays his usual grunting approval, which always annoys me by its laziness – its absolute refusal to take the trouble even to think about what's been done – and its acceptance of 'we'll get away with it' as the highest standard required. The idea of

making a film with him as producer – *All Neat in Black Stockings* – is really unreal.[28]

Mike Sarne, who would soon win a certain fame by luring Mae West out of retirement to make *Myra Breckinridge* (1969), almost tempted Lindsay with a script about a homicidal maniac, *Skinner*, to which Richard Harris had given approval. But Anderson's working relationship with Harris, by then, was beyond repair. The script he settled upon, and which he took with him to Poland, was a first script by a new writer called David Sherwin.

DAVID SHERWIN'S 'CRUSADERS'

Sherwin had been a Tonbridge schoolboy. In May 1960, aged sixteen, he and a friend, John Howlett, had written a script – 'Crusaders' – inspired in part by their schooldays, and partly out of admiration for a schoolfriend, Michael Mason. Mason, literary scholar and publisher, died in March 2003. Lindsay Anderson was sent the script by Seth Holt who, in 1965, had directed Bette Davis and Jill Bennett in the Hammer horror film, *The Nanny*. Encouraged by Anderson's interest, and with his first collaborator, John Howlett, in Rome working for Holt and unavailable, David Sherwin rewrote 'Crusaders' with his girlfriend, Val.[29] Its plot is as follows:

On route to school, Mick Travis, a senior pupil, bearded, shares a railway compartment with several people including a girl called Glenda. Mick pretends to be a Hungarian who fought in the Budapest revolution. Elsewhere on the train are other boys from his school, including Denson, who has been made Secretary of House Appearance and Haircutting (like Mick, he has an adolescent attraction for young Bobby Phillips) and Johnny Knightly and Mick have been passed over for promotion to prefect. At school, with the madness of term under way ('Run! Run in the corridor!') with dormitory and medical inspections ('ringworm, eye disease, music lessons, VD, confirmation class'), the Seniors mark out Travis as 'indecent'. Travis and Johnny sneak away from cheering at a college rugby match to go into town. At a riverside cafe they see Glenda, who works there, but who doesn't seem to recognise Mick. On return to school they are caught and, later, caned. Johnny receives three strokes. Mick is given ten. When Johnny is called upon to take part in the school racquets match, he changes his mind about covering for Mick, who plans to visit Glenda.

Mick: 'Just whose side are you on?'

Johnny wins the match and, at dinner, is awarded school colours. During the celebrations, Mick starts smashing dinner plates. Other boys join in. The seniors led by Rowntree stop the near-riot by slapping boys' faces. Travis is gated and told to report every hour to the prefect on duty for the rest of the term. Denson orders the school barber to shave Travis's head. And Mick keeps thinking about Glenda: 'We'll walk naked into the sea as the sun goes down. I'll make love once. Then die.'

In handicraft class, he makes Glenda a medallion and, unable to take it to her himself, asks Johnny. With Mick reporting hourly to Denson, Johnny goes to the cafe but hasn't the courage to talk to Glenda.

One night, the school is woken by a fire drill. Travis is ordered to take an extended cold shower for showing off by climbing down a drainpipe. Later in the term, Mick steals bullets and then rifles from the school armoury. He has a game of shooting with Johnny. At half term, Johnny is made prefect, and Secretary of House Punishments, to whom Mick now must report.

Annual inspection is taken by the general. On Field Day, Peanuts demonstrates the 'Yell of Hate' and Mick bunks off for a cigarette with Phillips, only to be caught and reprimanded by Johnny. Mick punches him. In the gym changing room, Travis is beaten, Phillips is dunked in the toilet, and the pair are 'married' by bullying seniors. With Christmas approaching, Travis climbs into the loft where the trunks are kept. He climbs out on to the snow-covered roof and curls up against the cold. At dawn, his body is found impaled on the school railings. School continues as before. Johnny goes to see Glenda. She is wearing Mick's medallion.

This was the film that Lindsay Anderson wanted to make. It had wit and invention and passion, but not enough self; changes had to be made. On 6 November 1966, writing from Warsaw, he outlined his suggestions to David Sherwin:

Dear David

Thanks for the phone call: and also for the new selection of notes. I have read again the two scripts I've got. Interesting, the first (dated 1960) is understandably a bit ... shall we say immature: bad on construction, and very romantic-sentimental in a touching adolescent sort of way. But some of its scenes are good material – Wallace and the talk about death – transformed later to Mick and Johnny: but I quite like Wallace:

perhaps there should be all three of them in this conversation ... Maybe
it's a pity to lose this Wallace altogether? I had an idea it might be he
who was after Bobby Phillips and ends up being expelled ... Willis and
his punishment shower: I know this becomes Mick: maybe usefully:
I don't know. It could be Peanuts, who remains to me an interesting
character, largely because of that telescope scene.

In the most recent script there is obvious improvement in construction; but I think we're agreed that too much has been lost in order to
achieve a tight narrative involving really only Mick and Johnny: and of
course there remains the basic flaw of Glenda, still entirely sentimental in
conception – and having become the basic subject of the whole story.

Apropos Glenda: it seemed to me that perhaps the best introduction
to her might be on the afternoon when Mick and Johnny cut loose from
the football match and go into town: using maybe the new motorcycle
idea: Johnny and the salesman chase after him: Johnny runs one way
and finds him: Mick yells, 'Get on the back' – and they ride off – they
both get carried away by the excitement – drive out of town and stop
at a transport cafe – where Mick makes mock-passes at the girl dishing
out the egg and chips: they hitch a ride back to town maybe in a truck,
leaving the bike behind ... and maybe later this is the misdemeanour
that catches up with Mick when the salesman and a policeman arrive
to interview his housemaster ...

Maybe Mick returns to the caff later: it could be when he's left alone
on the visiting day: and maybe Glenda seduces him ... anyway it's
having sex, probably for the first time, but not Romeo and Juliet.

It seems to me that the film should start at the school, and in the
school; because that is the world of the film; not coming into it with
scenes in the 'real' world first. For instance, the titles could be over
shots of the empty school, details of chapel, desks, gym, dormitories,
passages etc. with at the end a jump cut (for instance) from a deserted
corridor to it suddenly full of boys, shouts, trunks being dragged etc
... Now what about this warden. Actually I prefer the suggestion of
the headmaster in the first script: younger and specious I imagine.
Modern and 'enlightened': glib. Probably because he relates more to
my headmaster at Cheltenham. But this warden could be interesting
somewhere. Maybe he is the Chaplain? You have got a bit carried away
by him: but the book polishing idea could be good.

How can you possibly follow the explosion of the tree with a shot
of the Warden's wife passing the chapel in which is being sung 'The
Day Thou Gavest'? This doesn't make sense to me.

Dormitory scene with fat boy: good: worth fitting in if possible. Mick's clean teeth: looks to me like another red herring.

Narrow country lanes: first part good: including hair twisting. I don't know about country lanes: how do you visualise showing that he wants to be a Bedouin?

The pen knife: this becomes quite David Storey in its 'poetic violence'.

After Mick's expulsion: (much better consider exactly how he is expelled: and if) what on earth is Glenda doing here? She is very persistent. What a peculiar end to the film: is it the end? Seems to me nonsense: the point of the wall of death – if indeed we use it – but the idea was the sudden violence, the explosiveness of image and sound.

You have (excuse me writing like a school report) a fecundity of imagination, but it seems to operate rather without organic sense: like a series of prose poems: or jottings for a script. Sometimes a whole idea is valuable, sometimes a couple of lines, sometimes nothing.

What is really wanted, if not a tidy 'skeleton' is some idea of the progression: and some key scenes – instead of a plethora of peripheral imaginings ... For instance, do Stewart and Mick ever talk together? You remember you thought of using songs as some kind of linking device: I expressed scepticism: have you still a place for the school song? What about the speech, or Founder's Day celebrations, with the visit of the corporation members who provide an opportunity to demonstrate the social foundation and implication of the school?

Who are the principal characters? Warden: housemaster: wife: chaplain: what masters? Stewart – who else? Mick: Johnnie: Wallace: Peanuts: Stephans: Bobby Phillips: Barnes: Denson etc. The Girl.

I haven't mentioned, and I'm not sure if I should – what is the theme of this film ... Maybe it can't be put down on a postcard ... the image of a world: a strange sub-world, with its own peculiar laws, distortions, brutalities, loves ... with its special relationship to a perhaps outdated conception of British society ... its subjection of young minds to disciplines hardly related to the contemporary world; and to the domination of often freakish or deformed or simply inadequate 'masters'.

From the two scripts, and from the notes, I find it difficult to get an absolutely consistent picture of Mick, whom I take to be the principal character. I suppose I see him as a lively, independent, anarchic character; who arrives at the end at an act of violent, poetic protest ... But what precipitates this act?

An early scene, first waking day maybe, should show the music

3. *Lindsay Anderson directs the troops*

master teaching the new boys the school song. 'The New Boy' should
be a character. What is his name?

I don't very much like the juxtaposition of the naked HM's wife
with the military footsteps: isn't this a rather heavy symbol? (Maybe
it depends 'how it's done'; not heavy, aggressive tread.)

'Field Day': some misdemeanour here might precipitate a beating
for Mick. Anyway a funny and significant sequence is possible with
this material.[30]

On his return from Poland, Lindsay worked on the script with Sherwin. His main contribution at this stage was to encourage Sherwin to
break from the naturalistic structure and to reconceive the project in
terms of the epic, not the Hollywood epic but the Brechtian epic. In
August 1965, Brecht's Berliner Ensemble had taken London theatre by
storm with a season of Brecht's plays at the Old Vic. Lindsay befriended
the directors and actors, even arranging the last-night party:

28 August 1965: I took Manfred [Karge] and Matthias [Langhoe] back
to the theatre – where Hilmar [Thate] was by the stage door, in his
red shirt (British) and quite smart mod suit (German) ... After the

show – whose purity and vigour was stunning as ever – there was this ridiculous and awful muddle and graceless anti-climax – which ended fortunately in a smashing little party of our own. Ken Tynan's secretary had told me going into the theatre – 'There's a do in the dress circle bar afterwards' – and so, clutching my bottle of whiskey, I told Manfred and Matthias ... but they didn't know anything about it, and wouldn't go anyway as they'd not been invited – 'Let's go back to the studio' – so I went to see Hilmar – found him in his dressing room – all around actors lugging their things from the theatre – then over the tannoy came the belated announcement – drinks in the circle bar. Fuck that – we were leaving: but Wolf Kaiser caught hold of Hilmar and said politeness demanded ... so he went up: and I went out, sent the others off and promised to come on ... In the dress circle bar were sandwiches, champagne, drinks: practically no actors – [William] Gaskill and [John] Dexter – [directors at the Court] back from holiday and as camply brittle as ever. I got immediately involved in acid recriminations with a smooth girl handing round sandwiches – so superior in her Englishness she drives me nuts. I stuffed my briefcase and pockets full of crab and smoked salmon sandwiches – then we beat it to the studio in a taxi. And what a nice party we had! Egg and bacon: and *The Trial of Lukullus* which (bless them) they had given me: then singing and waltzing to our Scots record: and then we all sang 'Auld Lang Syne'.

I felt so at ease: amongst fellow artists: 'It's good for us you are here on our last night' Hilmar had said in the taxi – I am irredeemably sentimental of course. Manfred waltzing with Anne-Marie ('Lindsay – sing!') and Hilmar with Jocelyn [Herbert]. Happily the taxi we phoned for went away before we came down – so Jocelyn drove all back to their Carlyle Hotel. They invited us in for a drink – others were still sitting around in the bar. And we sang 'Mother Courage' songs: and Hilmar sang his Commune song – and 'Auld Lang Syne' again. Then out on the pavement and we all embraced with genuine emotion. I really miss them!'[31]

But when rewriting 'Crusaders', Sherwin's main influence would be the epic plays of Georg Büchner, *Woyzeck* and *Danton's Death*. A further model was Jean Vigo's 1933 forty-four-minute film *Zero de Conduite*, a semi-surrealist film about life at a boy's boarding school which ends with a speech day protest. In 1976, in an undated letter to a fan, Jack Landman, Lindsay Anderson explained Vigo's influence:

When I started planning the transformation of David Sherwin's and John Howlett's original script, 'Crusaders' into what eventually turned out to be *if....* – I did think about *Zero de Conduite*. Not of course from the point of view of reproducing it, or translating it into English terms – but at first most particularly in terms of structure.

When I first started working with David Sherwin, I was very conscious that we would have to try to construct a script in 'epic' terms rather than in the conventional narrative style which would be much more in the English tradition. It was in this respect that I thought of *Zero de Conduite* with its succession of poetic scenes, often without any particular narrative connection. And it was with this in mind that I had a special screening of *Zero de Conduite* with both David and John. I think that because *if....* does on the whole come off pretty well, people tend to forget not simply how unconventional is its content but also the way the film is structured. Certainly seeing Vigo's film gave us the idea and also the confidence to proceed with the kind of scene structure that we devised for the first part of the film particularly. (In the second half, of course, the narrative does become stronger.) I remember at a talk very early on – perhaps even the first time I met David and John – saying how the end of the film must erupt into a giant cataclysm. At first I think I had a vision of the college laid bare in smoking ruins!

Of course, interestingly, *if....* is very much more violent in its climax than *Zero de Conduite* ... Of course, too, sequences like the motorbike ride and the scene with the girl in the cafe have no parallels in *Zero de Conduite* – nor the scene under the stage with the discovery of the human foetus.[32]

With Sherwin back at work on the script, Lindsay continued to shuttle back and forth between London, Prague and Warsaw. In May 1967, in Warsaw, he made a twenty-minute film about a school – a music and drama class – *The Singing Lesson*. Scenes of the students singing songs are intercut with candid shots of everyday Polish life, so that the school serves in some way not as a microcosm of Polish life but as an oasis of human thought and artistic activity. The film ends with the Professor joining in the singing and dancing, much in the manner of Anderson himself at the finale of his 1973 film, *O Lucky Man!*.

CASTING AND PRODUCTION

In June 1967, with the script of *Crusaders* now in its final stages, it was taken up by Albert Finney's production company Memorial Pictures.

Finney himself was finishing off his first film as a director, *Charlie Bubbles*, written by Shelagh Delaney. Anderson and Sherwin went scouting for locations:

> 20 June 1967: David and I get away to Charterhouse. When we arrive I am momentarily struck by the compactness of its Victorian Gothic: an isolated fantasy world set amid rich green expanses on which white-flannelled figures are playing cricket. Momentarily I am again swamped by a tide of nostalgia for that youthful – celibate fantasy ... but it doesn't last long. The headmaster, Dr Van Ost by name (or similar), is a breezy eccentric, impatient and rather over-quick to demonstrate he knows exactly what its all about etc. – 'You want to shoot in winter? – The *Wuthering Heights* atmosphere I suppose ... ' seemingly quite ready to co-operate, pleased to suggest he could let us have 400 boys when we wanted them... The school itself – we were shown round by one of the heads of houses, a cool, complacent scientist, a confidently superior type without charm. The houses are unfortunately being renovated – but even the old one we saw lacked the spacious ugliness of Cheltenham. Much better than Dulwich, A or B+ ... As we left, David announced himself as feeling quite ill and intimidated by the whole experience... we recovered a bit with teas and Kit-kat and records on the juke box in a chara caff on the road home.[33]

In August, CBS agreed to finance the film. The headmaster of Anderson's old school, Cheltenham College, gave permission to film at the school – pending script approval. Knowing that this would not be forthcoming if he read of the bullying, the savage beatings, the cold showers, the 'tarting', homosexuality and the speech day massacre, David Sherwin rewrote the script. An in-office competition was held to find a title for the doctored script. The winner, Albert Finney's secretary, Daphne Hunter, suggested 'If' after the Kipling poem. David Sherwin put IF in capitals and inverted commas and added a long dash. Lindsay Anderson later reduced the title to lower case and added four dots. Sherwin's new and bogus script starts with 'Outline Notes':

> The film is intended to be a poetic, humorous view of life seen through the eyes of the boys. The film will show the general life of the school into which will be woven the lives, and also the adventure fantasies, of three particular boys – Mick, Johnny and Wallace.
>
> The overall effect of the film is to be lyrical – to show the reality of the world and its innate lyricism. To achieve this, and because we

are working outside the commercial framework of studio production, the film will be improvised. The following rough notes are an outline to aid the budgeting and logistical problems of the production.

1. The film begins with an evocation of the emptiness of the school buildings before the beginning of term. Lyrical shots of the grounds and the buildings seen through the trees.
2. The bustle and action of the beginning of term. Coming and going. The corridor is crowded with BOYS, shouting news and taking their trunks and possessions upstairs.
3. A crowd of BOYS reading the notices, discovering their teams and their new positions in the house. A new boy, JUTE, asks where he should go. A prefect, PETER ROWNTREE, gets a junior boy to help him with his books and sports equipment and asks another boy, BRUNNING, to show the new boy, JUTE, to the Junior Common Room.

Throughout the 'headmaster's script', Sherwin focuses on the lyricism – 'A small BOY carefully unwrapping tissue paper from peaches and arranging them in his locker' – and takes out all that may offend. 'Medical inspection' becomes 'The BOYS then line up to give in their health certificates'; the playful sword-fight in the gym ends before we get to 'real blood'; the savage caning of Travis and the Crusaders becomes:

ROWNTREE calls in WALLACE, TRAVIS and KNIGHTLY and addresses them. He tells them that he knows that they are wasting the most important years of their school life in mobbing around. They are supposed to be intelligent people and could get to university but instead are behaving like idiots. They may think that they are being very clever but they are behaving like children and should grow up or they will become the laughing stock of the whole house. He issues some kind of general punishment and perhaps orders them to go on Barnes's afternoon runs for a week.

The masterstroke of the headmaster's script was how Sherwin managed to keep in the speech day massacre, for the headmaster would be present on the day when the actors playing the Crusaders would be firing a machine-gun from the Cheltenham College roof. The problem was solved by breaking in two the first scene with the history master (Mr Stewart, played by Graham Crowden) and sticking the second half of it at the end of the film. In the complete history lesson scene, as filmed and screened, which comes about a third of the way through the revised script, Stewart arrives singing 'To be a Pilgrim'. He gives out the boys' essays and, failing to engage the class in a conversation about the growth of European nationalism in the nineteenth century, orders them to write a twenty-five-minute essay on George III. In the headmaster's script, this scene ends with Stewart's introductory talk about nineteenth-century nationalism (with the boy's apathy thus missing). At the end of the headmaster's script, after the Crusaders have set fire to the school and fired down on the fleeing speech day congregation, Mick Travis is stirred from this 'day-dream' by Stewart:

> *Mick is day-dreaming during the history lesson. He suddenly jerks awake when he realises that MR STEWART is asking him a question.*
> STEWART: Well, Travis?
> MICK: Sorry, sir. Er what?
> STEWART: It has been said of George the Third that he was 'a mollusc who never found his rock'. Said by whom, Travis?
> MICK: Plumb? J. H. Plumb.
> STEWART: Possibly ... 'What were the failures in the British Constitution and the political parties that prevented the mollusc-king from finding his rock?' A twenty-five minute essay ...
> *The CAMERA PANS across the BOYS' faces as they start to think, and one by one begin to write.*
> FADE OUT
> THE END.

JOCELYN HERBERT: The film was so funny, wasn't it? The headmaster was so real. And the real headmaster was always asking us in for sherry. I used to feel terribly guilty that we were betraying him, treating him very badly but Lindsay didn't feel anything like that. I said: 'Did you really show the headmaster the script?'
'Oh, yes, but of course I edited it.'
And there he was at the end, taking part in being shot! I'm not sure he didn't lose his job.

In September, CBS pulled out of the production of *if....* but Albert Finney had a fan in Charles Bluhdorn, the billionaire owner of the oil company, Gulf and Western. In October, Bluhdorn bought himself a Hollywood studio, Paramount and, without reading the script, agreed to finance the £220,000 budget.

The three remaining adult leads, the headmaster, the chaplain and the new undermaster, went to Peter Jeffrey, Geoffrey Chater and Ben Aris respectively. Anderson cast Jeffrey after seeing him play Macbeth at Brighton in a production which featured Patricia Healey, the star of *The White Bus*: 'He looked into my dressing room, and said a few nice things.'[34]

Chater was noticed nationally when he played Ingrid Bergman's husband in the 1965 West End production of *A Month in the Country*.

GEOFFREY CHATER: I have played a lot of establishment roles, and I try to show the man inside, the real man underneath the surface. I found that wearing the chaplain's clothes so much of the time on location helped me to get the feel of him. He has such overweening pride, and it is shown up in the most blatant way. I hugely enjoyed the part.[35]

Ben Aris is unlikely to have caught Anderson's notice as a child actor playing 'Tadpole' in the 1951 film of *Tom Brown's Schooldays*, nor as the title role in the Hammer horror film *Plague of the Zombies* (he played a zombie). When he asked at the audition what John Thomas, the new undermaster, was like, Lindsay replied: 'He's just like you.'[36]

BEN ARIS: The character has a certain reticence, a lack of push and shove that is very identifiable as me. But he's slightly more of a fool than I would like to regard myself. Also I'd like to think that I'd be less easily sucked into the establishment trap than he was.[37]

All that was needed now was to cast the boys. Auditions of professional actors started in late December 1967. Adverts in *The Times*, *Telegraph*, *New Statesman* and *Melody Maker* calling for 'Boys 12–19: Do you want to be a star? THIS IS YOUR CHANCE!', drew 5,323 amateur hopefuls to Marylebone Town Hall on the 1 and 2 January 1968. The boys were photographed holding books and guns, and asked to read from the script. From these open auditions only two boys were cast: Philip Bagenal, whose unusually pointed teeth won the part of 'Peanuts'; and Rugby schoolboy Hugh Thomas, who was cast as 'Decency' Denson, the general's son. As the search for boys widened to include professional actors, Brian Pettifer won the role of Biles, the boy who gets bullied:

BRIAN PETTIFER: I'd auditioned at Miriam Brickman's office in Half Moon Street, and had done further auditions at a theatre in the West End. This was in December 1967. I came down from Glasgow for the audition, which Lindsay thought was marvellous of me. He liked the fact that I was Scottish. He knew that English schools aren't filled only with English boys.[38]

Guy Ross was given the part of Stephans, the 'shag-spotted' senior. Ross began his acting career in 1963 as a gang leader in BBC2's *Story Parade* and, in 1965, played a precocious schoolboy in *One Night I Danced with Mr Payne*. *if....* was his first film.

MALCOLM MCDOWELL: I first met Lindsay Anderson in December '67. I was called by my then agent, the Hazel Malone Management, to audition for a film called 'The Crusaders'. I was asked to go to the audition during the day, when I was rehearsing the worst part in Shakespeare, Sebastian in *Twelfth Night*, at the Royal Court Theatre, a rather pretentious modern-dress affair. The director, Jane Howell, wouldn't let me go to the audition, because I was needed in rehearsal. Of course, I was never used. I rushed out and tried to make it across London by bus to get to the Shaftesbury Theatre. I came in late. Everybody was packing up and leaving. So I rushed on to the stage. Announced myself and was told to turn round, as if it were a cattle call. Turn round? I thought, what are they? Homosexuals who want to see my arse? I turned round. A young, vibrant, energetic man leapt onto the stage. He looked like a Roman senator. A little grey around the temples. Very kind eyes. He said: 'I'm Lindsay Anderson.' I did the reading for him. Very badly I thought, but he seemed to like it. He said: 'We'll let you know.'[39]

MIRIAM BRICKMAN (casting director): He [Malcolm] has a kind of eagerness and energy, which made him immediately a likely actor for the leading part in *if....* He also has a definite viewpoint. He has character, a sense of inquiry, perception, selection, a sense of rebellion. The camera picks up this kind of thing.'[40]

MALCOLM MCDOWELL: I heard that Lindsay Anderson was coming in to see the play. I was thrilled because he was obviously coming in to see me! Unfortunately, he left at the interval. Sebastian's big scene and only scene is after the interval. So he missed my big moment. Anyway, I heard from my agent that I was in fact down to one or two for the part and I was asked to go another audition.[41]

On 5 January 1968, Malcolm McDowell returned to the Shaftesbury Theatre (where Jimmy Edwards's Comedy Playhouse was playing). He found himself improvising a kiss in a cafe scene with fellow auditionee, Christine Noonan – Brickman had seen her in a class at the E15 Drama School – and being slapped hard across the face for his trouble. Not to be outdone, he fought back, and she gave as good as she got; soon they were wrestling with each other, pretending, at one stage, to be tigers. They tore up the script and were hired to play Mick Travis and The Girl.

MALCOLM MCDOWELL: That slap from Christine was the Zen moment in my life and my career, because that slap slapped me into reality. It slapped me into film stardom. Without that slap it would have been just an audition, but now I wanted to kill her. I stalked her around the stage. It was electric. I felt damn good and I thought I must be close to getting this role. I had been up for six where it was either me or Hywel Bennett, me or Michael York, me or somebody else and it was always them who got it – thank God! Because those films were such crap! This one turned out to be a masterpiece.[42]

On the same day, Lindsay Anderson cast twenty-three-year-old Robert Swann as the cane-wielding Rowntree. Educated at Pangbourne College, whose most famous old boy remains Ken Russell, Swann won a scholarship to RADA, toured schools in a Nottingham Playhouse production of *Julius Caesar*, featured in an old-time music hall show that played in St Louis and New York, cut two records singing Victorian songs, and graduated from *if....* by playing another head boy in Alan Bennett's play *Forty Years On*.

David Wood, an Oxford undergraduate, who played Wagner in the Richard Burton and Elizabeth Taylor production of *Doctor Faustus*; and Richard Warwick, an ex-Cheltenham College schoolboy, who played the part of Gregory in Franco Zeffirelli's film of *Romeo and Juliet*, won the roles of Mick's companions, Johnny and Wallace.

The role of the bully, Keating, went to Robin Askwith, who would go on to star in the hit sex-comedy series the *Confessions of ...* films. *if....* was his film debut. As he explains in his 1999 book *The Confessions of Robin Askwith*, he was cast because Lindsay Anderson saw him as Richard III in a school production at the Merchant Taylor school – improvising a line as his false nose melted under the lights: 'An iambic ad-lib, splendid Askwith ... The idea of a melting nose was such a clever metaphor. My name is Lindsay Anderson, this is the casting director, Miriam Brickman. We are making a film called "The Crusaders".'[43]

Casting the final 'Crusader', the pretty boy Bobby Phillips, was proving difficult until an unsuccessful candidate for the title role in Carol Reed's *Oliver!* arrived for a reading:

4. *The first take of the first shot on the first day*

RUPERT WEBSTER (Bobby Phillips): I was twelve years old and I wanted to be in the movies. I went to Holland Park Comprehensive and appeared in a few school plays, including a big musical production about the Wild West. I got the part in *if....* through a casting agent, Miriam Brickman. I was suggested to her by Roz Chatto, who was also a casting agent. I had auditioned for *Oliver!*, the film starring Oliver Reed and Mark Lester, but I was too tall for that. I had suddenly shot up. They liked me but I was too tall. I was casting about and I remember going in and reading for *if....*, not for Lindsay but for one of the assistant directors. He liked it and, straight away, he took me somewhere else, and Lindsay was there and I did the reading for him. I don't think the reading was with Richard Warwick [who played Wallace], it was with an older chap, but it was the scene where we were in the armoury together. I heard that day, or the next day, that I'd got the part. I was very excited.[44]

Filming started at Cheltenham College on 28 January 1968. The first shot, probably coincidentally and not a throwback to *This Sporting Life*, was of boys playing rugby.

BRIAN PETTIFER (Biles): I got off the train at Cheltenham, was taken immediately to be costumed, and then put right into the first scene, standing on the touchline of the rugby pitch! It was unheard of for an actor to 'act' on his 'travel' day.[45]

The college magazine, *The Cheltonian*, contained a pupil (Adam Mills's) account of the making of the film:

Any feeling of interest towards the filming was quickly dissolved in an uncheckable flow of acid comments from the new extras concerning the amount of time that they were required to put into it. For the first time in their lives boys complained of having to miss valuable lessons for which their parents were paying vast sums of hard-earned money! But, worse and worse, the masters were getting away with free lessons – righteous indignation boiled the blood! The first romantic imaginings of a glorious full-colour feature in *Photoplay* were fast replaced by the wave of anti-film opinion that swept College.

The third formers, though, were the first to participate, and within a few hours began to feel ten feet tall, as Mr Anderson poured profuse thanks upon them. Pupils soon forgot about valuable lessons and all too quickly academic work ground to a halt, while the cameras continued to turn. The threat, though, of the loss of two whole consecutive weekends was almost too much for some, and though only a few evaded their 'parts', the headmaster found that he had to remind us of our obligations to the film company ...

When the novelty of 'beardie-weirdies' invading the chapel to put up popish candelabra and lay down striking yellow carpets had passed off, some very boring hours were spent perusing books, papers and scrounged 'trash mags' to the beat of 'Good! Excellent! Now we'll have it again, please!'[46]

A call sheet belonging to Brian Pettifer for Saturday 16 March 1968, for three chapel scenes, gives a clear indication of the demands placed on the College. As well as twenty-six named members of the cast, there is a call for

Approximately 200 boys from Lower College to report to our costumes directly after Chapel (9.30 a.m.). After lunch those required for games are released. The remainder stay with us until 5.45. 20 Junior Boys required for Scene 47 from 7.00 p.m. to 9.00 p.m. Approximately 7 Masters and Wives from the College will be with us from 9.30 a.m. Other Extras: 16 Men to be Masters, to be on location at 9.00 a.m.

15 Women to be Masters' Wives.' The prop department was to provide College hymn books and psalters and a harmonium. Curiously, Robin Askwith is alone in being granted a lie-in. He needed to be on set only at 11 a.m.

At the same time as Lindsay started what would turn out to be a lifelong battle against the condescending hordes at Cheltenham, the editor, David Gladwell, moved into a cutting room in Bayswater.

DAVID GLADWELL: The director seemed to be reluctant to discuss the shooting script with me at the beginning, or to talk about editing ... At my first meeting with him, he made it clear that it would be he and not I who would be editing the picture and that my job would be to organise the cutting room ... All that he needs, apart from an adequate technician, is an ear to think aloud into at every stage of the process. So obsessed with perfection is Lindsay Anderson that even after the completion of dubbing he was still working creatively on it and several cuts were made to the master track itself. Ten weeks after dubbing he was still at work editing the trailer and publicity material. No stage was allowed to escape his control just as, during editing, no cut satisfied him until all the possible alternative arrangements of shots or alternative frames on which to cut had been fully considered.[47]

RUPERT WEBSTER: I stayed in digs with the guy who played Machin. There were chaperons and tutors. We had to carry on with our school-work, which was a giant pain. I thought it was going to be a nice long holiday. I remember going into the town a little bit, and having fun when we had some time off. I can't really remember what we did in the evenings. Some of the shoots started at six or seven in the morning. They liked to get us in early because of the light, so we were probably going to bed as early as they could get us to bed.

One of the first scenes I did was when I'm playing rugger with the new master. Unless you know I'm in there you can't really focus on me because I'm at the edges of the shots. I can't actually remember the very first scene I acted in, but I remember having quite a hard time with my entrance scene. I had to do a voiceover on that; my voice wasn't strong enough in the actual soundtrack. My mother was very pleased with the way the film came out. She thought my performance wasn't polished, that I wasn't 'a proper actor', but she thought I played it right for the character. I thought Lindsay was quite aloof with me. I thought he would work in closer, because he worked very closely with Malcolm

[McDowell]. I actually didn't feel that I was being directed as much as some of the other people. A lot of my performance seemed almost accidental really. Lindsay was always very nice and very courteous. Acting for him wasn't very taxing, though he did work other people quite hard. He had everybody's confidence.[48]

MALCOLM MCDOWELL: The shooting of *if....* was one of the most wonderful times of my life. There I was with this great man, master and pupil. The very first scene that I shot was with the three of us, Richard Warwick and David Wood. We were shooting the fencing scene in the squash courts. It was fun to do. We'd worked on it with the fencing guy from the National [Theatre] or somewhere. The next day, we saw the dailies and I was absolutely horrified because I'd done it naturally. My face was grotesque. It showed every wince and movement. I wanted to reshoot. Lindsay said: 'Malcolm, you've learned a good lesson today. You've got to be in control of every muscle in your face.' He was the master and I was the pupil. He never tried to make me play the role for sympathy. I hate that kind of acting. And anyway, Mick Travis wasn't the type to ask for sympathy. He makes his own decisions, and either you accept them or you don't. It's funny but the set of *if....* was very cliquey. Shooting was exactly as it was in the film. The three rebels and Christine hung together, and the small grotty boys kept themselves to themselves. It was just like school.[49]

DAVID WOOD: Whenever I asked Lindsay Anderson how I should react to a scene, he told me just to do what I would normally do in the circumstances.[50]

ROBIN ASKWITH: I struck up a friendship with Richard Warwick ... At night he would take me to the dubious downtown nightclubs in Cheltenham. We experienced our first 'joint' together. He was pinned up against a nightclub one night a little worse for wear ... We paid homage to Brian Jones [of the Rolling Stones], who came from Cheltenham. We stared at his house for hours one night.[51]

JOCELYN HERBERT: The only sets were the boys' studies. We built all of them and the Sweat Room. We'd build a section then regurgitate it as something else. Most of what you see in the film was already there. In the school we used the actual dormitories. I don't think we painted the dormitories but we may have painted the passages. We didn't do much in the school. We certainly built all the studies. They were all in a group, you see, and I made them so that you could pull the walls out not so you could take the camera in but take the camera to the wall. They were much too small to take the camera in. I hate that when you have an enormous space when it's meant to be tiny, and it worked perfectly. You could take out whichever wall you wanted.[52]

Filming at Cheltenham College ended in April, on the last day of the school term. In a wildly inaccurate memoir published in 1994, the headmaster, David Ashcroft, recalled:

I got really cross only once, on the last day of term, when the final shoot-out on the roof took place. It was quite a difficult scene to co-ordinate, and a long one, and it went on and on. They had to finish and daylight was going (though arc-lamps were always in use to deal with changing light). Then the bell for last chapel started to ring. Suffice it to say that chapel started only fifteen minutes late, but not to the sound of gunfire. So the term ended.

I received a letter from Lindsay dated 18 April 1968, from Paris. The Sorbonne riots had begun to be serious, and he wrote to say that as a result of what he had seen he thought he should 'turn the screw' a bit. No more. They did come back next term, annoyingly, to reshoot the rugby scene, but that was all.[53]

Was Lindsay in Paris during the student riots, and if so did this have an influence on *if....*? Probably not. The Ashcroft article is so riddled with errors as to be almost completely unreliable; furthermore, there had no been riots at the Sorbonne until May. Months of non-riotous conflicts between students and authorities at the University of Paris at Nanterre climaxed with the administration shutting down the university on 2 May 1968. Students at the University of the Sorbonne in Paris met the following day to protest against the closure. The Sorbonne administration responded by calling in the police, who surrounded the university and arrested students as they tried to leave the campus. When other students gathered to stop the police vans from taking away the arrested students, the riot police responded with tear gas. This was the first real act of violence. On 6 May 1968, the national student union and the union of university teachers marched to protest against the police invasion of the Sorbonne and were charged by the police wielding batons. Four days later, the riot police blocked a protest march on the Left Bank, prompting the crowd to throw up barricades. The police attacked at 2.15 a.m. leaving hundreds injured. Scenes of the students being bludgeoned by the police prompted a wave of international sym-

pathy for the protesters. More than a million people marched through
Paris on 13 May. Georges Pompidou, the prime minister, released all
arrested protesters and reopened the Sorbonne, but the protests continued. By the end of the week more than ten million workers, or more
than half the national workforce, were on strike. President De Gaulle
fled to the country.

Earlier in the year, there had been student–police conflict at New
York's Columbia University – the students protesting against racism and
the Vietman War; there would soon be violence on campuses in Japan
and Italy and Mexico. A new world order seemed to be emerging. But
Lindsay Anderson's film had been written almost six years earlier.

After Cheltenham, additional scenes, including the beatings and the
showers, were filmed at Aldenham School in Elstree, and at the Merton
Park Studios, London, where the filmed scenes included the discovery
of guns, mortars and a foetus under the school stage. In his book, *Going
Mad in Hollywood*, a fine memoir of his work with Lindsay Anderson,
David Sherwin recalled the following conversation:

> LINDSAY: Do you realise, that from this point on there's not one line
> of dialogue between the Crusaders? They say nothing for the rest of
> the film. Sheer laziness on your part.
>
> DAVID SHERWIN: It's called poetry, Lindsay – the poetry of the cin-
> ema.[53]

At the first screening of the film in England, in December 1968,
Lindsay Anderson took to the stage afterwards and told the audience:
'The rest is up to you!'

if.... was marketed with images of the film locked inside a hand-
grenade, by which stood Mick and Johnny holding machine-guns and
asking the question: 'Which side are you on?' Lindsay Anderson hadn't
set out to make a film 'about' student protest. But he had made good
his long-term goal 'to combine a present-day theme with an authentic
picture of features of English life all too frequently misrepresented by
the movies'.

TWO
The Narrative

When planning the press publicity for *if....*, Lindsay Anderson wrote a long interview with himself, asking himself the questions he expected the press to ask. The first question was: 'What would you say your new film is about?'

A: That's a horrible question. I don't think one can ever say what one's work is 'about' – certainly not if one has managed to make anything of value. You see one doesn't set out to make a film 'about' anything. One starts with an impulse and a subject and an area of experience, and whatever one makes grows out of that. It is for the critic to decide what it's 'about'. All I can say is that it's a story that takes place in an English school, a public school. It's set in the world of boys, of three boys in particular, and it uses that peculiarly hierarchic world to dramatise issues of authority, tradition and freedom, with, I hope, a sense of humour. I suppose what attracted me to the subject first of all was the sort of nostalgic feeling most people have for their schooldays. They are such an important, formative part of one's life, that anything one makes on this theme must be extremely personal. The other aspect that appealed to me, I think, was the extent to which a school is a microcosm – and particularly in England, where the educational system is such an exact image of the social system. I like very much to show a little or a limited world which has implications about the big world and about life in general existence.[1]

He closed the interview with:

Q: Finally, there has certainly never been a film that shows English public school life which such directness as *if.....* How do you think it will strike audiences who know nothing of these places?
A: I should have thought that such an intimate and authentic picture of these great and influential establishments would be appreciated by anyone interested in the way the world works. (Which I believe most

5. *Ben Aris leads the juniors in a game of rugby.*

people are.) And anyway, it is not a film about public schools, any more than it is a film about a public school. It is a film about law and disorder, about freedom and responsibility, about love and the denial of the heart. Now, you see, I have answered your first question.

And, in between, he explained all that he thought necessary to explain about the film. He wrote that the film was 'prophetic': ' ... forecasting the shape of things to come – the conflict between established tradition and youthful independence that is evidently breaking out all over the world. This seems to me one of the functions of an artist, perhaps the most important function, to prophesy. As the most important function of a critic is not to judge, but to interpret.'

Q: I see the film as an illustration of the consequences of people blinding themselves to reality – society pretending that the real facts of life don't exist. Is this a valid impression?
A: I suppose it's valid. But, again from my point of view, I would never use a word like 'illustration'. Perhaps to you the film may be an illustration. To me, it isn't. I would hope that it's an experience, not an illustration. Certainly people should be able to draw from a film like

this what they like. One of the marks of a good film, or a good work of art, is that it is susceptible to being interpreted in a variety of ways. This shows it has the richness or ambiguity of a real experience, that it isn't in any way a tract. But that is one interpretation you might put on it. Somebody who has completely different values from you might say it was an illustration of the ruinous effect of irresponsibility and over-lenient treatment of the young.

if...., Lindsay Anderson's film set in the world of boys, and 'about law and disorder, about freedom and responsibility, about love and the denial of the heart', is certainly open to interpretation. It is a film in eight distinct parts, each part indicated, in the Brechtian manner, by a title card. In a 1990 letter to a fan, Rupert Wyatt, who wanted to adapt the film to the theatre (his school), Anderson explained that the eight titles were in the script but not originally filmed: 'Think of Brecht (as perhaps we did when we used those titles. The film was first edited, as a matter of fact, without them, though they had been in the script. Then we realised that they would be extremely useful.)'

THE FILM: CHAPTER 1

The film starts with a monochrome shot of the Paramount mountain, indicating that it was made with American money. An organ plays the intro to the College hymn. When the male voices sing the opening line: 'Stand up stand up', the following appears in white letters on a black background:

> Wisdom is the principal thing:
> therefore get wisdom:
> and with all thy getting
> get understanding.

This is identified (in red letters) as being from Proverbs IX 7. Black, red and white are the colours of the film's advertising poster. Black and red are the colours of anarchy.

With the first verse drawing to a close, a long-shot still-photograph of College, taken from the cricket pitch, comes on to the screen. The College buildings take up the upper third of the frame. The bottom two-thirds are black, over which rolls the credit – 'A Memorial Enterprises Film' (in white) – '*if....*' (lower case, four dots, in red; with copyright notice in a much smaller font in white) – 'introducing

MALCOLM MCDOWELL, DAVID WOOD, RICHARD WARWICK, ROBERT SWANN and CHRISTINE NOONAN' (in white). More cast members, and crew's names appear; the picture of College remains unchanged but the soundtrack changes. We hear documentary sounds, doors slamming, children laughing. With the credits continuing to roll, the documentary sounds fade and we hear the first bars of Marc Wilkinson's music score: a woodwind tune singing through a discordant frame of plucked strings. Then comes the chapter heading 1 (in red) 'COLLEGE HOUSE – Return' (white on black). The inclusion of chapter headings is possibly a borrowing from *Zero de Conduite* but more probably it's a steal from the Judy Garland musical *Meet Me in St. Louis*, which Anderson adored, which begins with a monochrome still of the house where most of the action takes place, and which uses different views of the house as chapter headings throughout the film (the monochrome turning into full colour as the 'still' comes to life). The three-part 'overture' of sound is taken in form from Lindsay Anderson's favourite John Ford film, *They Were Expendable* (1945).

The most striking thing about the opening sequence that follows is that we are plunged headlong into the innate lunacy and surrealism of life in a British boarding school. The opening shot is of a corridor full of uniformed schoolboys juniors in short jackets, seniors in tail-coats. There is a lot of pushing and shoving and shrieking and shouting. The keen observer will notice that in the background of the corridor, centre right and centre left of the frame, two young boys, filmed in profile, are facing each other and talking to each other across the corridor. They appear to be about seven feet tall, or suspended in the air. The frame is so busy that it's easy to miss them. One's attention is quickly taken by a small boy jumping on to a wheeled trunk pulled by a senior – the camera low to the ground so that we are not looking down at the boy. We see a full double line of boys going up and down a staircase. The boys going up are carrying trunks and suitcases. The boys coming down are carrying the paraphernalia of school life – musical instruments, sports equipment – one boy is reading a book. Back in the corridor, two boys collide. A tin of baked beans spills from the trunk-tray carried by one of the boys. In anger he speaks the film's first words, a shout of: 'Machin, you bloody shag!' Machin uses the tin as a makeshift puck.

The boy who spoke first is Markland, played by Charles Sturridge, who would go on to become a film-maker and direct *Brideshead Revisited* (1981).

Rowntree (Robert Swann), the head of the house, enters from on high – imperiously – walking downstairs, his back to the camera. It is no coincidence that the first we see of him is his cane. At the bottom of the stairs he turns round – the camera tracking a few feet to the left, almost unnoticeably because it tracks at the pace at which Rowntree moves. We see Rowntree's face. He shouts: 'Run! Run in the corridor!' Which is exactly not what we expected to hear.

The delicious subtlety of Anderson's technique, not only in this opening sequence but in the whole film, is a wonder to behold. Nowhere in the film does the camera draw attention to itself or distract attention away from the scene or the players. Likewise, the material (the situations, the performances, the dialogue) is so strong and so striking that the viewer's attention does not drift away to 'looking' at or for the technique. Throughout the film, the placing of the camera, and the choice and the length of shots, is masterly. Anderson's camera technique could be described as Chaplinesque but there is little in Lindsay Anderson's film writings or diaries to suggest he was a real admirer of Chaplin. Anderson's camera style lacks the playfulness of the films Ondricek photographed for the Czech New Wave, and it isn't really Fordian. It lacks the open-air grandeur of Ford, and the chiaroscuro dramatics of John Ford cameramen such as Gregg Toland, Joseph August and Arthur C. Miller. It lacks too the rigorous prettiness of Winton C. Hoch, whose colour films for Ford include *Three Godfathers* (1948) and *The Quiet Man* 1952). If there was a blueprint for the subtle camera technique, it would be Yasujiro Ozu, and in particular Yuhara Asuta's work on *Tokyo Story* (1953). In the winter 1957 edition of *Sight and Sound*, within the context of an article about contemporary Japanese cinema, called 'Two Inches off the Ground', Lindsay Anderson wrote:

'Movies have got to move.' One of the things these Japanese directors have made clear to us is that our interpretation of this precept has been a great deal too facile. They [the Japanese] almost persuade us, in fact, that movies are best when they don't move at all. More seriously, they oblige us to reconsider and redefine what we mean by movement. (And here, it is interesting to note, their calm example seems to confirm the most interesting and daring ventures of Western avant-garde work in recent years.) For in the West, 'cinematic movement' had usually been related to our experience of the theatre, in effect if not in style. Cinema is not literature.

In the second part of the article, he focused on *Tokyo Story*: 'In *Tokyo Story*, the camera moves only three times from the beginning to the end of the picture, and then with the most gentle discretion.'[2]

This 'gentle discretion' is a cornerstone of the Lindsay Anderson film style.

Almost eight years later, when *Tokyo Story* was released in London in March 1965, Lindsay Anderson was enraged by Dilys Powell's suggestion that the film wasn't 'great' because her response to it was 'respectful but dry-eyed' – it failed to move her. His letter was published in the *Observer*:

> Sir – May one suggest, with all deference to Dilys Powell, and to several other 'respectful but dry-eyed' critics, that their failure to commend Ozu's *Tokyo Story* may be caused by some misunderstanding of the way great art works? It is surely a little trivial to imply that the value of a play or a film or a poem is to be measured by the number of handkerchiefs it moves one to soak ... It is impertinent to suggest that a critic is, or should be, something more than a piece of emotional litmus paper[3]

As the first sequence in *if....* progresses, the camera picks up on Jute (Sean Bury) a new boy. In his first scene he is sneeringly patronised by his fellow pupils, most notably by a senior, Stephans, and a junior, Biles. We soon learn that Stephans and Biles are the two least popular boys in College House. By being rude to Jute, they both spurn the chance of making a 'friend'. In this dog-eat-dog environment, it is better to bully than to be bullied. It's more satisfying taking a step up from the bottom and to push someone else down than to offer kind words and a helping hand. The psychology is true.

It is the tradition of 'school stories' for the 'new boy' to be the main focus of the film; the one through whose eyes we learn about the school and become conditioned to its strange traditions; the one who, in the final chapter, has found his feet, made an impact and risen to the top. For a short while, *if....* merrily plays along with this fantasy but, importantly, after the film's first quarter, Jute becomes less and less significant. He is sucked into the system so much so that he almost 'disappears', reduced to a non-speaking 'extra' on the edge of the frame, until he emerges again at the film's finale, carrying an altar piece, a puppet in the Establishment charade.

Jute is taken to the junior boys' common room, or the 'Sweat Room'. Interestingly, at the centre of the first shot of the Sweat Room, we see a boy making a collage of pictures cut from magazines; another boy is idly swinging a calendar; the picture on the calendar, an autumnal scene, is brilliantly clever shorthand to denote the season in which the film is set. Collage making seems to be the boys' only creative or expressive outlet. The pictures in the Sweat Room are mostly of undressed women, as one would expect from newly pubescent boys, but on the side wall, black on red, is the famous portrait of Che Guevara. To emphasise this, the poster is repeated black-and-white, in a subsequent five-second shot, prominent above a blond boy who is sitting on a desk and holding a rugby ball. To the left of the image of Che Guevara, squeezing into the left of the frame, is a superb full-portrait poster-photo of Geronimo, the Native American freedom fighter. Running along the top of the wainscot is a sequence of pictures of a motorbike, not unlike the one ridden by the rebel author of *The Motorcycle Diaries* (Guevara), and very much like the one Travis will later steal for a joyriding romp in the countryside. The full strip of motorbike pictures is partially obscured by the rugby ball held by the blond boy. None of this – the design, the framing – is accidental. Travis, the revolutionary, the freedom fighter, steals the motorbike when he should be watching the College rugby match. Collages on very different themes are found in the rooms of the seniors.

The first Sweat Room sequence ends with a shot of young Markland taking tissue-wrapped peaches out of a box, sniffing them deliciously, and placing them with artful care on his desk. Such sensuous scenes play an integral part in forming the film's atmosphere. It's not an 'angry' film made by a dissident; it's a beautiful film made by a man who enjoyed his schooldays.

The film's hero enters after Rowntree has gathered the 'scum' (juniors) together, ordered Markland to warm the lavatory seat for him (a wonderful piece of madness from the original script) and fixed Jute up with his 'Bumf Tutor', an experienced junior who will teach Jute all there is to know (and which must be learned) about College. From the corridor, the film, and Jute, progress to the Sweat Room, the junior common room presided over with an authority that is both admirably and distressingly adult, by a little boy called Machin: 'Silence in the Sweat Room!' This is a world where communication has been reduced to shouts, orders, commands, snatched whispers.

The time is ripe, both dramatically and actually, for a hero to come to sweep all of this away. But first, as in all fairytales, comes the 'love interest'. In Sherwin's original script, the love interest (allbeit puppy love) was between the hero and a junior called Bobby Phillips. In the film, Bobby Phillips enters down the stairway taking all manner of verbal bullying in his stride: 'Come on up, Bobby ... We want to stroke you.'

At the very moment Phillips leaves the frame, the hero – Mick Travis – enters at the point where Phillips left. The boys are no longer lovers, but it is clear from this that they are somehow linked. They are two of the five 'crusaders' who will be firing down on the school at the finale. Swathed in a black hat, with a black scarf covering his face (an allusion to Hitchcock's *The Lodger*) and hiding behind a suitcase carried on his shoulder, Malcolm McDowell as Mike Travis strides in and up the stairs. After a quick visit to his dormitory to deposit his trunk – a refreshingly heavy bounce as it's dropped on to his bed; no movie-empty props here – and a short comic scene with 'Peanuts's ray-gun', Travis takes his trunk-tray containing his more personal items to his study. The contents of his tray tell us a lot about his character: a fighter-pilot's helmet, a photograph of Marilyn Monroe, a map of the world, a photo-spread of motorbikes, motorbike goggles, books, records, a magazine, sellotape, toy handcuffs, a string of human teeth, and something red, white and blue that may be a Union Jack.

Johnny Knightly, the third Crusader, enters Mick's study through a red-curtained partition above the door. In the frame he is framed against a portrait of Chairman Mao. As Mick shaves off his summer-grown moustache, a poster of a motorbike racer by the mirror, Knightly takes the teeth from Mick's tray, then a magazine. He holds the magazine open at a photograph of a muscular man firing a machine-gun, and asks: 'What do you think of him?' Travis replies: 'Fan-tas-tic! Put him right in the middle.'

Johnny tears out the photograph and tapes it to the wall by a picture of Edvard Munch's 'Scream' and a photograph of three soldiers. None of the images is there by chance.

The next scene is in the College Hall, where we meet the fourth Crusader, Wallace, invited over to stand with Mick and Johnny. We also meet Keating, the bully, played by Robin Askwith. On a first viewing, Askwith doesn't seem to be in the film much, but when one learns that Anderson had him on the set every day, and one looks again, we see him often, at the edge of the frame – an established Jute. Here he starts a non too subtle game of English whispers, a variation on the Chinese version in that the words are spoken loudly for all to hear: 'Biles, why are you a freak?'

Silence descends on the room as the Whips (coloured-waistcoated prefects) enter – preceded by a cane-carrying Fortinbras. The absurd, elitist, procession of honour is completed by Mr Kemp, the housemaster (Arthur Lowe), his wife, the nurse and a new teacher, the undermaster. The staff are introduced by a shot from on high – slightly above the heads of the boys and looking down. Mr Kemp makes a welcome speech: 'We are your new family. And you must expect the rough and tumble that goes with any family life ... ' It is followed by an angry demand from Rowntree, who complains that last term, the house got a reputation for being 'disgustingly slack'. 'If there's any repetition of that deplorable lack of spirit ... I shall come crashing down on offenders.'

From these very unlovely 'pep talks', and to the sound of a bell, the boys line up for medical inspection. The first active role played by one of the film's three main female characters is the nurse (Mona Washbourne) indicating for a boy to take down his trousers. With a torch in hand she bends down to look at his genitals – the very image of a sex-starved loon. The three leading women in the film, the nurse, the housemaster's wife, and The Girl, are all conceived in terms of sex. The Girl is liberated; the two staff members are sexually repressed. It's a pity that the manifestation of the nurse's repression (a dream of her making love to the boys) was cut from the final film.

From here to the seniors cleaning their teeth in readiness for bed. Keating, the bully, draws attention to 'Fatso's blubber'. 'Fatso' is played by Richard Tombleson, who later worked as the location manager on *Britannia Hospital*, the third and final film in the Mick Travis trilogy. Earlier one noted that the College colours as seen on the boys' ties and scarves (and later on their rugby kit) are the colours of the Union Jack – red, white and blue – for the College stands as a microcosm of Britain (with the Scots boy, Biles, the target of the English bullying). Here, the viewer is surprised by the bright yellow silky nightclothes of the three Crusaders, Mick Travis, Knightly and Wallace (bounding athletically over a partition to join in the fun with 'Fatso'). The dormitory leader, the unloved and officious Stephans, naturally wears a dressing gown that is red, white and blue.

This dormitory scene is intercut with the sight and particularly the sound of the prefects announcing and carrying out junior and senior dormitory inspections (their instructions shouted in fine theatrical unison) and also by a delicious scene involving Mrs Kemp (played by Mary MacLeod) and the new undermaster (Ben Aris). The Kemp/Aris attic scene is perhaps the most acutely observed, delicately played and perfectly realised scene in the whole film. It says everything there is to say about the loneliness of living in 'digs', and of take-the-money landlords (although Mrs Kemp is almost certainly not the landlady here, she is acting the 'type'). The 'polite' offers of companionship are quite intentionally dismissed by a tone of voice that is as hard and cold as the room itself, and by the fact that she asks for and takes a shilling from the tenant to operate the gas meter. The hard rattle of the coin landing in an empty metal tin serves as the scene in sound in miniature. These adults, the undermaster and the housemaster's wife, are products of the system they're now employed to maintain. They have been raised to accept confinement, and to make polite but insincere allusions to friendship. As Evelyn Waugh wrote in *Decline and Fall*: 'Anyone who has been to an English public school will always feel comparatively at home in prison.'

This attic scene is the first in the film in monochrome. It has entered film folklore that the interchanging between colour and black-and-white (monochrome) was the result of the film-makers 'running out of money' – which is nonsense. Lindsay Anderson's explanation is given in his foreword to the published screenplay:

> When Shelagh Delaney and I were working on the script of *The White Bus*, which was also a poetic film, moving freely between naturalism and fantasy, I remember suggesting that it would be nice to have shots here and there, or short sequences, in colour (it was otherwise a black-and-white film). The idea also appealed to Miroslav Ondricek, and we did it. Almost no one has seen *The White Bus*, but I like the film very much, and I think the idea was successful.
>
> It was this precedent that gave me the assurance – when Mirek said that with our budget (for lamps) and our schedule he could not guarantee consistency of colour for the chapel scenes in *if....* – to say, 'Well, let's shoot them in black-and-white.' In other words it was not (of course) just a matter of saving time and/or money. The problem of the script seemed to be to arrive at a poetic conclusion, from a naturalistic start. We felt that variation in the visual surface of the film would help create the necessary atmosphere of poetic licence, while preserving a 'straight', quite classic shooting style, without tricks or finger-pointing.
>
> I also think that, in a film dedicated to 'understanding' [as denoted by the caption at the start of the film], the jog to consciousness provided by such colour change may well work a kind of healthy *Verfremdungseffect* [alienation effect], an incitement to thought, which was part of our aim.
>
> And finally: Why not? Doesn't colour become more expressive, more

remarked if drawn attention to in this way? The important thing to realise is that there is no symbolism involved in the choice of sequences filmed in black-and-white, nothing expressionist or schematic. Only such factors as intuition, pattern and convenience.[4]

The chapter ends in the senior dormitory after lights out, with Stephans being taunted and with a bit of adolescent talk about sex. The final line of dialogue is spoken by Peanuts: 'Paradise is for the blessed, not the sex-obsessed.' This is possibly taken from the Alan Ladd film, *Wild Harvest*, which Lindsay had seen as an undergraduate at Oxford. He'd been taken aback by the violent image on the film's poster, a fist wrapped in a chain. It was still in his mind days later:

> 20 April 1947: As I walked up from the Cambridge, I found myself repeating not the Wordsworth which I had attempted unsuccessfully to learn on the way, but Alan's lines: 'Paradise is for the Blessed/Not for the sex-obsessed.'[5]

CHAPTER 2: COLLEGE

A quote added to the title card reads: 'Once again assembled ... '

Over the sound of the communal singing of the hymn 'To Be a Pilgrim' is played a fine montage of views of College, and of boys inside the chapel. The scenes and views outside the chapel are in colour; those inside are in monochrome. We see most of the 'charactered' boys, including Jute trying to find the right page, and we see most of the staff, including Mr Stewart, the history master, singing with one hand holding a hymn book, the other hand easy in his pocket. The female staff stand hatted on the balcony.

Service ends with a Buxtehude organ voluntary. Outside the chapel, boys stream out and collect their bags and books piled by the door. From the headmaster's bright and breezy patter, we learn that Rowntree spent the summer in India, the country of Lindsay Anderson's birth. Was Rowntree inspired by someone Anderson knew from his time there, in the army perhaps in the Second World War? It is more probable that the line was thrown in as a reference to the British Empire, for Rowntree is certainly a man who would like Kipling's 'If'. We see boys jostling beneath a covered walkway, their playful shrieks probably the same ones used in the film's overture. Then comes the history lesson; this is a brilliantly written scene, but its greatness is in the staging, and the playing.

6. *Lindsay Anderson rehearsing the juniors including Rupert Webster*
   (far right)

The first shot is taken from within the room and, of course, there
is no movement by the camera. The doorway is framed on the left by
a boy sitting on a desk and, on the right, by Keating at the master's
desk, his hands on a pile of books (a symbol of his future ambition).
The class, led by Denson, enter in single file (the scene opens at the
moment Denson enters the classroom). Keating tosses a book to the boy
across the room, which goes between Denson and a boy improbably
called Pussy Graves, who comes to the front of the frame and complains
about the ban on girls from Springfield being in the school orchestra.
Behind Graves is Stephans. At the moment when Graves has finished
speaking, he has turned round and almost completely moved out of
frame; the viewer's eye is now on Stephans, sitting on a desk and facing
the camera (i.e. away from the entrance and away from the blackboard).
Travis walks in and makes a sarcastic comment to Stephans. At the
back of the frame, filling in the compositional gaps between Stephans
and Mick, two other pupils are looking on and laughing. Within this
scene, the focal point and the action have changed three times but the
camera hasn't moved once.

As dialogue passes between the boys, we hear Mr Stewart singing 'To be a Pilgrim'; the boys stop talking and look to the door. The camera cuts to an internal corridor and we see Stewart, in academic gown, riding a bicycle. The comedy of the scene is enhanced by the timing of the cut as he enters the classroom, and by the immaculately smooth timing of the two boys who take the bike from him, park it and close the classroom door. The magnificent nonchalance of the two 'bike' boys and the non-reaction of the rest of the class to this grand entrance, tell us that such an occurrence is commonplace. There is something of Harry Davenport's role in *Meet Me in St. Louis* in the singing entrance of the old man.

On his arrival, Stewart strides across the room, slapping and rubbing his hands, to open wide the two windows nearest his desk. He turns and, with a fine theatrical flourish, returns the boys' 'holiday essays' by calling out each boy's name and tossing the essay to him. All this is done without edits, and with the camera panning once to the left and once to right (the movement masked by Stewart's marching).

The themes of the lesson are nationalism, imperialism, war and monarchy. At the time of Anderson's and Sherwin's schooling, and indeed at the time the film was made, history in English classrooms was restricted to the history of great men.

With the boys settling down to write a 'twenty-minute essay without notes', after Travis has established that he is smarter than Denson, who doesn't know what a mollusc is, the scene cuts to the chaplain teaching a junior maths set. This scene starts and finishes with shots of a window. The chaplain strides around the silent boys and pompously dictates formulae, hard-slapping one boy across the back of the head for no reason other than that it amuses him to and that he can use the slap as a punctuation point in his speech. With his speech continuing (the entire scene plays without a single cut), he stands behind the new boy, Jute, slips a hand into Jute's shirt and twists the boy's nipple. To the present-day schoolboy these scenes seem fantastical, but they were commonplace in schools in 1968. So much so that this scene was not mentioned by the Cheltenham College headmaster (or any contemporary reviewer) in the list of complaints about the finished film.

From the maths lesson to a lesson on life given by the headmaster as he takes the prefects on a walk around College. This short scene contains one of the most effective shots in the film: a long-shot of the headmaster and his prefects walking from left to right across the outside of the chapel. The shot is marked (and made both thrillingly

real and surreal) by the unmoving presence of the groundskeeper. In
flat cap and long coat, he is standing in profile with one foot on the
arm of a bench, one hand behind his back, and one hand holding the
steering bar of the immobile sports-line marker. Naturally, the group
passes him without comment. The headmaster's talk is about middle-
class morals and values, which include huge sacrifice in war (we see a
platoon of schoolboy soldiers march by) and education: 'Education in
Britain is a nubile Cinderella, sparsely clad and much interfered with.'
This facetious prattle, which makes the boys laugh politely, and which
is intended only to make the speaker sound modern and clever, comes
mostly from a then recently published book written by the headmaster
at Eton, sections from which are quoted verbatim by the staff in the
film. The headmaster's lesson concludes with: 'Britain today is a power
house of ideas, experiments, imagination, on everything from pop music
to pig-breeding; from atom power stations to mini-skirts, and that's the
challenge we've got to meet.' Anderson and Sherwin didn't know it
yet, but the headmaster had just outlined key elements in the film they
would make next: *O Lucky Man!*

After a high-shot looking down on small boys quickly setting out
cutlery in the dining room, framed by close-up portraits of old school-
masters, this 'College Education' chapter continues with Jute being
tested and forewarned by his 'bumf tutor' Brunning (a red-haired,
bespectacled boy next seen playing a schoolboy in John Krish's 1968
film of Waugh's *Decline and Fall*) and by a second boy, Markland. To
add an edge of claustrophobia and urgency, the scene plays in close-ups
of the boys' faces, the camera angled slightly down on poor Jute. One
word wrong and he fails the test and the two boys teaching him get
beaten; and Jute has to take the test again. It's all a part of the theme
of repression, Byzantine rules and codes that form a part of a repressive
regime that forbids visits to the town and leaving the house after dark,
and which now fills free time with forced nonsense and fear. In this
scene, the innocence of Jute contrasts beautifully with the frustrations
of the two more experienced boys.

The scene changes. On the soundtrack we hear, for the first time,
the singing of the liberating and divine 'Sanctus' from a *Missa Luba*
recorded by a Congolese choir, and we see a close-up of a detail of
Travis's study. Two-thirds of the frame is taken up by a detail of a
collage of photographs on the wall; one-third by three full shelves of
schoolboy clutter – artfully arranged and all telling us something of
Travis's character. The central image of the montage, fit for a per-

formance of the Sanctus, is a Catholic dignitary, hands raised and looking to heaven; around him are grouped images of war, including the photograph seen earlier of the man firing a machine-gun. With a cut, the view changes to Travis stretched out on his bed and adjusting the controls of the record player playing the Sanctus. He repeats the introductory bars – stopping the Mass when it moves to a passage of hard African drumming. He cuts out more magazine pictures for his wall. The picture in his hand, and which now falls to the floor, is of a lion. We will learn why, later.

The recording of the Sanctus was made by Les Troubadours du Roi Baudouin, a Congolese choir, with percussion section, consisting of about forty-five boys (aged nine to fourteen years) and fifteen teachers from the Kamina School. Sherwin and Howlett used to play the record (released on the Philips label), when they started work on the script. Additionally, three years before making the film, Lindsay Anderson recorded in his diary a visit to Richard Harris's house:

> 5 December 1965: I was welcomed, came into the hall: and Richard came down the stairs ... He offered me a drink ... I inspected the layout: the same 'dentist waiting room' – with the dining room now full of Mexican purchases – chairs, wrought-iron candelabra, an antique wooden sideboard. This prompted me to ask if my coat (of my suit) had ever come back: 'Oh yes' says Elizabeth – 'we wondered whose it was ... ' (so much for one's presence in the thoughts of those about whom we think) ... Richard takes me up to his study to show me his record player-cum-tape machine – expensively fitted into an antique Mexican chest ... he puts on three records – a Mass.[6]

A charismatic anti-hero playing music from a Mass on his record player. At this time, Harris was Anderson's inspiration. The sight and the sound would have stayed with him.

There is a very marked contrast between this gentle scene of Travis in his study (if images of war and a brief burst of violently rhythmical and percussive music can be called 'gentle') and the scene that follows. At once we are assaulted by the wild screams of boys, and Keating in the gym wielding a whip. A little gang, comprising of Keating, Pussy Graves and two juniors are chasing Biles. The shouts and screams of these boys is the English school equivalent of the African Sanctus – the percussion here is played by the crack of the whip and the sound of the pole-end of a broomstick being banged on the floor in quick attempts to hit Biles's feet. When Biles is captured, with Keating giving the 'playtime' equivalent of what we learn later is the 'Yell of Hate', he is carried to the lavatories, stripped of his trousers, inverted over and into the toilet bowl and left there, tied up and helpless. The scene is coloured further by the fact that the lavatory cubicles are without doors – all part of the school's dehumanisation process. One of the cubicles is occupied by Wallace strumming his guitar. Perhaps the guitar is there to make it clear that the soundtrack is intended to be the English school equivalent of the African school music of the earlier scene, but it is more likely to have been included because, in this context, it is real and funny. Wallace talks down to Biles as he helps him down. He doesn't offer him words of sympathy or comfort. Boys like Wallace don't have and don't want to have friendships with boys like Biles. The scene ends, again with Biles's unexpected line, beautifully delivered: 'Excuse me, please, you're standing on my clothes.'

The chapter ends with a short scene in the chapel. The juniors are being coached in the school song, as elsewhere in the building, the chaplain listens to the sexual confessions of Stephans. Needless to say – for there isn't a false note in any part of any performance in any scene of the film – the playing by Geoffrey Chater here is magnificent. His left hand clasps his chin, fingers nervously stroking his lips, his eyes and his half-whispered words betraying desire. His ringed little finger and the gold cuff-link on his crisp linen shirt speak volumes about the fine material life he has for himself here. The tentative hand which he reaches out to place on Stephans's head we know, from his earlier scene with Jute's nipple, is not really a touch of friendship or comfort.

CHAPTER 3: TERM TIME

The undermaster, amusingly dressed in white shorts and a tweed sports jacket, and making a sound one could associate with a huntsman directing a pack of hounds, is taking the juniors in a game of rugby. He picks up the ball and runs with it, is soon caught by the boys, and with laughter and respect is pulled playfully to the ground.

A monochrome shot of the college at evening, and a scene of the nurse returning the boys' laundry (an essential part of school life always neglected in other school films) acts as a prelude to the important scene in this chapter: the tempting of 'decency' Denson with the boy beauty of Phillips, played by Rupert Webster. It takes place in the senior common room, a room hung with a collage of sporting prints. The sports played in this room are boy-watching and the tempting of Denson.

7. *Anderson explains the finer points of Rowntree to Robert Swann*

The scene begins with a close-up of the back of Phillips (it is not too unconventional for a scene about 'the temptations of beauty' to start this way). By Phillips's head is a fine piece of carved English oak. Phillips raises a hand to hold on to the oak and the scene cuts back to reveal that he is kneeling by an open fire, toasting muffins. He is watched left and right by Rowntree and Denson respectively, and from the back by a third senior, Barnes (another fine pictorial composition). The three seniors, all watching Phillips, are pretending to be otherwise engaged. Two of them are reading; Denson, most obviously looking at Phillips, is drinking tea from a china cup. Phillips, castigated by Rowntree as 'a sod' and 'a lazy little bugger' (gay sex terms) for bringing the wrong food, is dismissed from the room. On his way out he passes a fourth, hitherto unseen, senior, Fortinbras, whom the camera now follows as Fortinbras tosses aside the newspaper he was pretending to be reading, to announce: 'He gets a little lovelier each day!' Ensuing talk on 'homosexual flirtatiousness' is dismissed with a swagger of condescension by Denson, whose hypocrisy and 'decency' is put to the test by Rowntree. Rowntree goes to the door and calls for Phillips, who is told he will be 'scumming for Denson from now on'.

RUPERT WEBSTER: A big scene for me was when I'm knocking on Rowntree's door. I had been called back to be Denson's 'scum'. Denson is trying to 'maintain standards' but really he 'wants' this boy. It is actually quite a good scene. There's a lot going on there, although at the start I'm on my own and all I do is knock on the door and move my hair out of my eyes. Lindsay said to me: 'This is going to be your scene.' I was the only person in the shot. I had seen him direct other actors and they had to do it time after time after time and I thought: 'Oh, crikey.' I did the scene twice and he said: 'Perfect!' I was so thrilled. I didn't know about the whole scene, in which one of the prefects says: 'Oh, he seems a little lovelier each day', until I watched the movie, and I thought: 'That's outrageous!' I wasn't told I was going to be the pretty boy character. I don't think I was ever shown a full script. It was very much under wraps. We were told it was 'adult' but we weren't really told what the story was. I think we were all quite protected ... I think the only scene I ever got a little bit concerned with was when I had to get into bed with Richard Warwick. I had no idea that was coming. I thought: 'God, what else am I going to be asked to do?' But it was so innocent. And Richard was such a nice chap. I took my Uncle to a screening in Knightsbridge just before the film opened in the West End. Afterwards he said: 'My goodness, that was a hell of a movie!' He was really quite shocked. But he enjoyed it.[7]

The next scene takes place in Mick's study, again introduced by a still life, a shot of another part of the collage and the magnificently naturalistic and yet artful arrangement of 'props' on a shelf. The wall photographs (which include face photos peering from within the bookshelves) are almost all of attractive women, some nude, with a bullfighter thrown in to add the element of violence. The conversation throughout the scene is mostly of sex and violence; adolescent boys theorising, talking nonsense and showing their complete lack of understanding of the opposite sex: Wallace says: 'What makes me nervous about girls is, you never know what they're thinking.' Knightly replies: 'I don't think they do think.'

The first person we see in the scene is Johnny. He is reading a horoscope (Lindsay Anderson was fascinated by horoscopes). He tells Mick of the need to resist the urge to go into battle this month. Mick, wearing his string of teeth and writing in a notebook, spouts a bit of adolescent poetic nonsense about death, takes a swig from a vodka bottle and passes it to Wallace, who is looking at himself in the mirror and fretting about going bald and having bad breath.

Before taking a sex question prompted by the magazine Johnny is reading, Travis announces in mock-poetic phrasing: 'There is no such thing as the wrong war. Violence and revolution are the only pure acts ... War is the last possible creative act.'

Densons enters (centre), the camera tracking back gently to frame him between Johnny and Mick and leaving Wallace in the centre facing him, thus echoing the framing of Bobby Phillips being 'grilled' by the fire. But in this case the one to whom all are looking has the power. Denson orders the three boys to their feet and to take their hands out of their pockets. A two-minute cold shower in the morning is doled out because he thinks their hair is too long. He confiscates Mick's string of teeth and calls him a 'degenerate'.

A ringing of bells, and a morning montage of College buildings takes us to the next day. Phillips, carrying a tin bowl of hot water and a towel, enters Denson's room (his wall pictures are of school, religious and military scenes – including a photograph of his father, General Denson, who arrives at the end of the film). Denson opens an eye, half fearful, half lustful, as Phillips prepares the shaving cream. Later, sitting upright in a bathtub, drinking tea and waited on by Phillips, Denson, the very picture of imperious condescension, takes a madman's pleasure in keeping Travis under the cold water for much longer than is his due.

CHAPTER 4: RITUAL AND ROMANCE

It starts with a song, boys singing a psalm, followed by Rowntree reading from the Book of Deuteronomy – 'That ye may live and go in and possess the land, which the Lord God of Fathers giveth unto you' – one of the passages used by the British as a justification of imperialism. This scene is in black-and-white, as is the scene which follows (started with a whistle). The linking shot is a colour detail from a stained-glass window, which Mick, in the chapel, is looking up at. Perhaps this is to suggest that he's the only one in the place who sees things in colour, i.e. as they are; or perhaps it is suggesting a 'vision'. The meaning becomes clearer when we identify the image on the window he is looking at, a young person returning a sword to its sheath, as Mick's namesake, the Archangel Michael. Beside the archangel is pictured an old man, bearded to the navel and carrying a staff – the very image of the 'wise'. Get wisdom and with all thy getting get understanding. The only victory in this school will be through war.

From the 'ritual' of chapel, to the ritual of shouted PE instructions

8. *A helping hand for Sean Bury as Jute*

as juniors are ordered to execute a 'through vault'. At the end of the exercise, with the boys ordered to 'get their sweaters', the scene turns to 'romance' as Bobby Phillips, standing on the balcony of the gym hall, watches Wallace perform on the high bar. The danger in this desire is denoted by the percussive edge of Marc Wilkinson's score, which comes to the fore for the first time in the film. In *if....* music is used properly, i.e. only when there is a dramatic purpose for it. After the introductory vibrato, and the camera tracking from Phillips's viewpoint, to and over the edge of the balcony, the tension in the music is eased by a sustained harmonious chord on the strings. Phillips isn't the only boy watching Wallace (actually Sergeant Instructor Rushforth is the body-double who performs the gymnastic twirling); Machin and Biles are watching too, but Phillips's eyes meet Wallace's. Wallace performs almost like a peacock in courtship. All the boys in the scene are wearing white, like the acrobatic boys in Vigo's *Zero de Conduite*, who somer-sault bare-bottomed in a cloud of white feathers. And like the scene in Vigo's film, Wallace's exhibition plays in slow-motion. The 'romance' is broken by the harsh-sounding shout of the PE instructor ordering the juniors back to the house. Phillips lingers, briefly.

9. Malcolm McDowell and David Wood at play

The ritual and romance theme continues in the next scene, with Wallace joining in with Knightly's sword practice and the two duelling like heroes in a romantic novel. Mick Travis swings in on a rope, like a character played by Errol Flynn. The romantic flavour becomes Romantic as Byronic quotes are thrust forward with swords: 'War – even unto the knife!' ('War, war is still the cry, "War even to the knife!" ' 'Childe Harold's Pilgrimage' Canto 1, 86).

'England awake!'

'Give me another horse!'

'We are not cotton-spinners all ... Some love England and her honour yet!' (from Tennyson's 'The Third of February 1852').

The last quote, shouted by Mick at play, could serve as a reason why he does what he does at the end of the film. The school (which is England) has ground you all down, but not me. I'm not of your England, I'm of the real England, and I'll fight until its true values are restored.

Wallace shouts 'Death to tyrants!' and the pretend battle spreads into an adjacent room, the film returning to full colour as the three boys burst through the door. Here, two on one, Mick is backed into a corner and beaten. The 'real blood' on his palm balances the visual composition with the red silk in the handle of Wallace's sword.

Another close-up of an ancient oil painting and we are at a dinner table. Around its edges, a crowd of senior boys. At the head, looking fearful, and all but mute throughout the scene, is Mrs Kemp, teased with rude smiles and, by Mick, with the suggestive rudeness of a phallic-shaped bottle of sauce: 'Do you need this, Mrs Kemp?' Women to these boys equal sex.

The food, served up with a proud smile from the nurse – quite hilarious in the context, for the food looks awful – is a colourless stew. In the next scene we see the nurse on the touchline of a rugby game which Rowntree has ordered all to attend. 'Fight! Fight! Fight! College! Fight!' she spits, with clenched fists and hate in her eyes. She's the very model of a psychopath.

Mick and Johnny aren't at the rugby match. They've escaped. We see them in long-shot, the zoom picking them up, running into town across a roundabout and cheekily stopping the traffic. Ironically, for this scene of 'freedom', they are locked together by Mick's toy handcuffs. A sweet brief electronic chime on the soundtrack, which then clears of all but 'documentary' traffic noise, provides a frame to the 'fantasy' unrolling in the street as the boys mime a sword fight or, perhaps like James Dean in *Rebel without a Cause*, they're fighting with razors. Mick is admonished by a bold and public-spirited pedestrian as Johnny dies on the pavement. The pedestrian's rather too unusual costume, a headscarf, bare legs and a hugely expensive fur coat, suggests, alas, that she's an extra.

When the scene cuts, the 'enhanced' natural soundtrack is replaced by a repeat of the electronic chime, as a three-shot montage takes us inside a motorbike showroom. Mick steals a motorbike. With Johnny riding pillion, they take to the countryside. Here Wilkinson's score and Anderson's camera – point-of-view shots from the front of the motorbike, tilting up to look through trees to the sky – are at their most expressive. They are free from the confines of college.

Mick and Johnny stop. They walk through a doorway (another through-the-door sequence that changes into black-and-white). Condiments on the tables to the left of the frame tell us that we are in a cafe. The soundtrack rumbles with the 'desire' theme we first heard in the Bobby Phillips balcony scene. The two boys walk to the serving hatch which, like the rest of the cafe, seems to be empty. A knock on the counter brings in the film's third female character: The Girl (Christine

10. *Christine Noonan publicity still*

Noonan). She is as two-dimensional as the women who have gone before her, but she's their opposite, she's young, she's cool – sliding the coffee cups down the counter like whisky glasses in a Western saloon – and, in marked contrast with Mrs Kemp, she responds to Mick's sexual advance with a thunderous slap across his face.

After comically, sourly, defiantly loading his coffee cup with sugar, Mick walks away. Wilkinson's 'desire rumble' plays on the soundtrack as he approaches the juke-box. He makes his choice. The selected record plays and, of course, it's the Sanctus from the *Missa Luba*.

The Girl approaches him, a hand on his shoulder, challenging eyes, strange poetic words and a replay of the actors' audition scene. When the choral sequence in the Sanctus progresses into rhythmic African drumming, we recall the photographs of African lions on the floor of Travis's study (where we first heard the opening bars of this movement), as Mick and The Girl play big cats, growling at each other, pretending they've got claws and, finally, rolling around naked on the floor together. The nudity was McDowell's suggestion.

MALCOLM MCDOWELL: When we came to shoot the scene in a cafe off the A5, it was going very well. I sidled up to Lindsay and I said, 'Lindsay, don't you think it would be great if, when we are writhing around on the floor, there is a cut and we're naked?' Lindsay said: 'You ask her.' 'Christine, Lindsay has just asked me if you and I would mind rolling round on the floor naked.'[8]

Bystanders in the cafe were asked to leave. But Malcolm recalls 'getting up off the floor and looking out at a whole line of lorry drivers looking through the windows'.[9] In an interview with the *Sunday Telegraph*, Christine Noonan, who had the power to veto the scene after seeing it at rushes, recalled: 'He was stark naked and I was stark naked, but we were both so busy fighting that I can't remember what he looked like in the nude.'[10] She said she agreed to do it because she felt that it was 'in context for the whole film', a moment of youthful liberation, an acting on impulse.

Thereafter, after a shown game of paper–scissors–stone, the film returns to full colour and we see the three riding on the motorbike, The Girl standing between the two boys, her arms raised in joyful celebration as if worshipping the pagan sun. In 2004, in Edinburgh, at his one-man show 'Lindsay Anderson, a Personal Remembrance', McDowell recalled Lindsay telling him that this image was the one that came to him when he first set about visualising the film.

CHAPTER 5: DISCIPLINE

It is dark outside. The camera is outside, looking down through an upper window at juniors at work in silence in the Sweat Room. The only sound we hear is Rowntree's footsteps hard on the wooden floor. Again, we see him first from the back, and we see his cane before we see his face. The scene, now black-and-white, cuts to a shot of another high window, then to a shadowed figure shining a torch. It is Denson on duty rounds. He sees and talks to the undermaster who is working under his car. A bell tolls and we are inside the armoury, where Wallace and Bobby Phillips are smoking. Bobby is talking; Wallace, the senior, is listening. It's the first 'civilised' exchange between a senior and a junior in the film. Phillips says he wants to emigrate to America and become a criminal lawyer: 'I believe in having a goal … That way you succeed.' He challenges Wallace about his lack of ambition, and adds to a question about his mother, that he doesn't think she's married to his new dad: 'I don't mind at all about that sort of thing.' This 'courtship' is interrupted by the snooping Denson. Wallace ushers Phillips into hiding and covers for him.

The scene cuts to Travis's study, again introduced by way of a close-up of the photo-montage on the wall. It is a closer detail of an area of the wall we've seen before, the raised hands of the Catholic at the bottom left of the screen, and the machine-gunning soldier at the centre bottom. After a long sequence in black-and-white, the film has returned to full colour, but the only colours in the photo-montage are the battle greens of a soldier's uniform and the violent red-orange of a fire. The jump back into colour (and these violent images) is enhanced by the brassy discords of Wilkinson's score now playing on the soundtrack. From the photo-montage, the camera cuts to a close-up of Mick struggling for breath, his head inside a plastic bag. A hand enters the frame and pulls the bag off him. It is Johnny holding a stopwatch. Wallace is also in the room, watching. The boys talk about the 'most horrible way to die'. Mick suggests 'being flayed alive – that's what the Crusaders did to their enemies', thus planting the seed of a violent action being plotted by these present-day Crusaders. The talk descends to childish (slightly forced) laughter, and we cut to a very formal dinner party at the housemaster's apartment. Naturally, in this context, the wife is reduced to the role of servant. Around the housemaster's table are the prefects. Rowntree talks about 'a lunatic fringe', seeks permission to stop College getting a 'reputation for decadence', adding that 'unruly elements threaten the stability of the house. It is best to nip them in the bud.' Permission is granted for Rowntree to do what he thinks best. The scene ends in close-up on the housemaster (Arthur Lowe) avoiding his prefects' eyes. He picks up a slice of fruit from his plate and chews on it – a splendid portrait of an inadequate man.

The sound of boys singing the final verse of a hymn takes this scene to the boys' dining room; Rowntree is flanked by the nurse and Mrs Kemp; before them are white tea cups and iron cooking trays full of sticky buns. The hymn singing finishes. Rowntree says grace – efficiently and without feeling. The boys collect a sticky bun – silenced by Rowntree striking a bell, once, and saying 'As soon as you have finished, juniors to the Sweat Room, seniors to their studies ... and wait in silence.' The boys continue the push to get supper. Mrs Kemp admonishes a boy who takes a second bun with the nasty hard-edged tone still commonplace in English schools.

As the juniors settle nervously into the seats in the Sweat Room, and the voice of Rowntree shouts the names of 'Knightly! Travis! Wallace!', we see Peanuts take his seat in his study. His study walls are covered with astral photographs – an eclipse, multiple images of the rings of Saturn – and a series of pictures of a human embryo. This, together with the 'Stargate' sequence that follows later when Peanuts looks into a microscope and sees cells dividing, is Stanley Kubrick's film *2001, a Space Odyssey* in miniature. Coincidental? Probably. Kubrick's film was released in London early in May 1968. Anderson had certainly seen it by 1970, by which time Kubrick had seen *if....* four times and cast Malcolm McDowell in the lead role of *A Clockwork Orange*. The shot of the cells dividing can also be read as a metaphor for the violent action that follows – the caning of the Crusaders – violence begets violence. The war has begun.

Following Rowntree's shout, the next sound we hear is the hard sound of the Crusaders' shoes on the wooden corridor floor. Shots of the three boys walking to and from the senior common room frame the scene in the common room. Much of the chapter's sound-dynamic from this point onwards is told in the sound of footsteps, in particular the sound of Rowntree's run-up in the gym as he beats the Crusaders with a cane. In the senior common room, backed by his crowd of prefects, Rowntree tells the boys he is going to beat them for being 'a nuisance ... a danger to the morale of the whole house'. Travis's verbal response, a truthful and eloquent tirade, can only make things worse: 'The thing I hate about you, Rowntree, is the way you give coca-cola to your scum, and your best teddy-bear to Oxfam, and expect us to lick your frigid fingers for the rest of your frigid life.' This speech closes on the tightest close-up in the whole film, Rowntree's face, stung and contemptuous.

The greatness of the sequence that follows is the perfect fusion of pictures, performance and sound, and Anderson's know-how of where exactly to place the camera and what to do with it when it is there. The Crusaders and then the prefects enter the gym hall changing room; the prefects walk through the changing room and into the gym through the left side of the double doors at the far side of the room. Wallace is called into the gym and caned – four strokes. The swift run-up and slow walk-back sounds of Rowntree's shoes on the wooden floor frame the ferocious whip-slap-crash of each thunderous cane stroke and 'tell' us all we need to 'see'. Wallace returns. Knightly is called – and caned. When he is being caned, Wallace, who on return to the changing room has been jumping on the spot and shadow boxing, lowers his trousers and asks Mick to see if blood has been drawn. Mick affirms that it has. Knightly returns dishevelled from his beating. As he returns to the room, Travis, at the bottom of the frame, is as far from the doors as he can be and yet still be in the frame. At the moment Knightly closes the door behind him, Travis marches with an arrogant confidence to the doors and arrives at them at the moment his name is called. With a thrilling swagger, he pulls open both doors, left door in his left hand, right door in his right. All of this, the entire scene – two hundred seconds long – has played without edits and with the camera from a fixed point at the back of the room looking down at the boys. There is a camera movement – a lateral panning shot – at the start of the scene when the Crusaders enter the room but, as usual with Anderson, the movement is masked by being at the same speed at which the object, i.e. the boys, moves within the frame.

We cut then to the gym-side view of the changing-room door and Mick, smiling with rude health and confidence. When he was preparing to star in Kubrick's film *A Clockwork Orange*, he took the script to Lindsay Anderson:

MALCOLM MCDOWELL: I really didn't know how to play Alex [in *A Clockwork Orange*]. I was very nervous about playing it. I knew it was a great part but I wasn't quite sure what I should do with it. On the Sunday before the Monday we started shooting, I got a call from Stanley. He said he had mumps. I was so happy, not happy that he was ill, but relieved that I had another week to prepare. I took the script to Lindsay and asked him for advice. He read it and said: 'Thank God I'm not directing this!' I said: 'That doesn't help me.' He said: 'All right, Malcolm. There's a shot of you in *if....*, a close-up, when you open the doors in the gym, there's a nice close-up of you and you have this look, this smile, on your face. That's the way you play this part.' And I went: 'Lindsay, thank you.' It was a masterful piece of direction. He had said something I could understand and knew how to do. And it gave me plenty of room to play with. It was a blueprint for the performance.[11]

After being ordered to take up a degrading position on the gymnastic bar halfway down the room, Travis is given not four but ten full-blooded strokes of Rowntree's cane. After the second stroke, the soundtrack stays in the gym (the sound of the beatings continues unabated) but the camera cuts to a tracking shot of the frightened faces of junior boys in the Sweat Room. A physical punishment of three boys is taking place, but it is psychological torture for all. The juniors are innocent of whatever charge Rowntree has jumped up for Wallace, Knightly and Travis; but punishing innocents was an accepted and encouraged part of English school discipline at the time. The punishing of innocence is a foundation stone of imperialism. We see a close-up of Stephans, his pen in an ink-well in his study. Before the tenth stroke falls we see Peanuts looking through his telescope at the cells dividing.

MALCOLM MCDOWELL: When he was directing me in *if....* his agenda was 'get Malcolm's confidence and I'll get what I want'. He created the atmosphere in which I could act. And he does it so well that you don't even know he's pulling the strings. An example of a brilliant piece of direction he gave me was in the beating scene, which I think is one of his favourite scenes. When I get up, I wipe my eye, but with my back to the camera. That's Lindsay. Just this movement of the arm, from the back. He is so brilliant. Acting is all about movement. Most actors don't move ...[12]

The chapter ends, of course, with the unexpected: Travis accepting Rowntree's hand and thanking him. Like the scene of the undermaster in his new lodging, this is all part of the falsity of English 'good' manners. A picture of a system where a 'thank you' said with sincerity could mean 'I hate you'.

CHAPTER 6: RESISTANCE

Like Chapters 2 and 4, Chapter 6 starts with the sound of boys singing, and with a short montage of College buildings. The boys' song here is the College song, with solo treble. After another shot of a school window, we are in a classroom, a library, a senior Greek class presided over by a pipe-smoking old gentleman in strange dark glasses. Fortinbras reads from and then translates a passage from Plato's *Republic*, which includes the prophetic phrase: 'And do you not remember, I said, that we also said that we must conduct the children to war on horseback ... ' (the duty later of the chaplain himself).

From this talk of children and war the scene cuts to Mick's study, but not via an introductory shot of the pictures on his wall. The film cuts straight to a Mick in close-up, a smoking cigarette in his mouth, a gun in his hand. He fires a shot – a pellet. Wilkinson's music starts on the soundtrack, the woodwind theme that was used over the credits. Mick is sitting on his bed. The lid of his record player has been closed and is serving as a table on which he keeps his cigarettes and ammunition. As he reaches out to reload, the camera cuts back smoothly to show the record player. Above it on the wall is a photo-portrait of Lenin in his Polish cap. Mick fires at the photo-montages, at the breast of a nude model (a colour picture) pinned in the midst of a black-and-white photograph of riot police; a dog; Audrey Hepburn and partner; a man in bed with his wife and child; a nude girl's bottom; a man whose arms are raised in submission; the clockface of Big Ben; two glasses of Martini (the red-topped darts wittily serving as cherries); a man framed through the window of the Queen's golden coach (*the* symbol of the innate surrealism of the British Establishment). The frame jumps forward to a closer look at the shot figure.

It's been clear from the start of the film that Malcolm McDowell, in his film debut, is not only a film star, but a great film actor. The key to spotting great acting on film lies not so much in recording how well lines are spoken, but in watching actors when they are not speaking. Can the camera read the thoughts conveyed by their faces? The scene of Malcolm as Mick taking pot shots with his pellet gun is film acting of the highest calibre. Look at how he uses his body, his hands, his arms, his eyes. It's a scene without words because it doesn't need any words. Mick Travis's words are few and far between from now on.

From Mick in his silence we cut to Rowntree talking with pomp and pride at winning the Bigley Memorial Marathon Chalice, the cup carried in by little Jute. Rowntree orders the boys to celebrate by performing the 'House Thump', a sort of Anglo-pagan equivalent of the Africo-Christian drumming of the *Missa Luba*. From the 'House Thump' the scene changes back to Travis's study. Again the entry shot is of the photographs on his wall. Lenin at the centre-bottom of the frame is crowned by the soldier firing a machine-gun, and above him the fire. The camera pans down, past one of Robert Capa's famous photographs of the American landing at Omaha Beach, to Mick, head back, swigging one of the last drops of vodka. Real bullets are produced. A pledge is taken, palms cut open, blood to blood. Mick's words are few and mostly monosyllabic. The 'mouthy' youth is becoming a man of action: 'We're on our own now ... Trust me ... when I say ... Death to the oppressor ... One man can change the world with a bullet in the right place.' He says the last line with the camera closer to his face than it has ever been in the film. Over his shoulder, partially obscured by Mick and out of focus, is the photograph of Lenin. Mick moves out of shot. The focus-puller brings the photo of Lenin into full focus. 'Real bullets.'

From Travis handing out the real bullets, the scene changes to perhaps the funniest sequence in the film, a three-element bedroom sequence which starts in the housemaster's bedroom and which takes in the nurse and the junior boys' dormitory. The housemaster, sitting upright and cross-legged on his bed, is singing. His wife, sitting up in a back-draped twin bed, plays an accompaniment on the recorder. It is infantile, sterile, charming – realism heightened for poetic effect. The music is joined by a fairy-like theme by Marc Wilkinson and the scene cuts (with a jump that indicates some footage has been cut – see 'Cut Scenes' at the end of this chapter) to the camera closing in on the nurse. She is lying back in an armchair, head back, eyes closed, left hand stroking the top of her breast, now rising to gently stroke the leopard-skin pillow behind her head – a lover's smile on her face. The camera moves in to a close-up and is now tracking past the beds in the junior boys' dormitory. The music is the 'desire' theme we heard when Phillips and Wallace first looked at each other. The camera stops by Phillips's bed. Wallace is in bed with him. Both boys are asleep.

Allison Graham, in her 1981 book *Lindsay Anderson* observed that the scene in the housemaster's bedroom could be a visualisation of the opening paragraphs of Lindsay Anderson's famous 1957 essay 'Get Out and Push!':

> Let's face it: coming back to Britain is always something of an ordeal … And you don't have to be a snob to feel it. It isn't just the food, the sauce bottles on the cafe tables, and the chips with everything. It isn't just saying goodbye to the wine, goodbye to sunshine … For coming back to Britain is also, in many respects, like going back to the nursery. The outside world, the dangerous world, is shut away: its sounds are muffled. Cretonne curtains are drawn, with a pretty pattern on them of the Queen and her fairytale Prince, riding to Westminster in a golden coach. Nanny lights the fire, and sits herself down with a nice cup of tea and yesterday's *Daily Express*; but she keeps half an eye on us too, as we bring out our trophies from abroad, the books and pictures we have managed to get past the customs. (Nanny has a pair of scissors handy, to cut out anything it wouldn't be right for children to see.) The clock ticks on. The servants are all downstairs, watching

TV. Mummy and Daddy have gone to the new Noel Coward at the Globe. Sometimes there is a bang from the street outside – a backfire, says Nanny. Sometimes there's a scream from the cellar – Nanny's lips tighten but she doesn't say anything ... Is it to be wondered at that, from time to time, a window is found open, and the family is diminished by one?[13]

if.... is a film about breaking out of the nursery.

The scene which had changed to black-and-white as it entered the dormitory stays black-and-white as the camera tracks the night sky. Peanuts, looking through his telescope, is joined by Mick – both boys in their dressing gowns. Peanuts talks but Mick doesn't. Mick hands him a 'real bullet', perhaps an invitation to join the Crusaders. Peanuts turns the bullet over in his hand, looks at it, and gives it back. He invites Mick to look through the telescope. Mick lowers it and sees The Girl leaning out of a window and combing her hair. She waves back. All heightened realism turned into film poetry.

CHAPTER 7: FORTH TO WAR

This too starts with an exterior of a College building – the chapel. On the soundtrack another reading from a Bible chapter that seems peculiarly English: 'The Son of God goes forth to war ... a kingly crown to gain.' The speaker is the chaplain, whom we see – in black-and-white – when the scene cuts inside the building. He is high on his pulpit, looking down, in more ways than one, at the congregation: 'We are all corrupt. We are all sinful. We are all meat to be punished,' he says. 'If a soldier fails to do his duty he expects to be punished.' We now see his congregation: a school full of boys all dressed as soldiers. The chaplain's tirade continues on the themes of betrayal, desertion and merciless punishments – all fittingly self-pleasurable for a man who enjoys hurting little boys. As his speech finishes, ending on the word 'deserters', he leans forward as if to spit it at the boy who has turned round to look at him – little Jute.

The sounds of drums – English military drums, not African drums – take us outside the chapel, where the chaplain, now in the full guise of an English army captain, and riding a huge horse, leads the marching boy-soldiers past the chapel, into the road, and onwards to the battlefield. From afar, Anderson's camera watches this strange procession, now joined by the sound of buglers; the camera eye unchanging as line after line of boys march past – in their midst an armoured car. The bugles stop but the drummers keeping drumming as the scene changes. We are inside the empty school, a lovely montage: a deserted corridor, names carved on a chair, sports kit in sunlight on the gym floor, the housemaster's wife, Mrs Kemp, walking naked through the school. Outside the school, the loud drums are joined by the crunch of booted feet marching on tarmac. This heightened sound continues as we cut back inside the school to Mrs Kemp now running a hand over the steel sinks in a boys' dormitory. She picks up a bar of soap and fingers it as one would something precious. She picks up a towel, holds it to her breast and looks over her shoulder.

Now we are in woodlands. Boys running. The sounds of gunfire and whistles. Denson orders Travis, Wallace and Knightly to go on ahead to attack and destroy a tree. The scene that unfolds is shown from Travis's clear, questioning perspective. Everywhere the lunatic surrealism of the English playing at war: the undermaster blowing his whistle and redirecting them through, not round, a thorny thicket; Peanuts teaching juniors the 'Yell of Hate' ('It's the yell that counts. Everybody back'), an allusion perhaps to the 'Two Minutes' Hate' which citizens of Orwell's *Nineteen Eighty-Four* have to perform; a screaming platoon of boys attack a large crumbling shed, explosions all around them. Later, in a seemingly quieter area, the boys encounter again the excited lunacy of the undermaster announcing his re-arrival, lighting and tossing a blank hand-grenade at the Crusaders and shouting with glee: 'You're all dead … I've won!' The chaplain, a disdainful look on his face, trots by on his high horse. Mick looks at the chaplain with equal disdain, and he takes off his beret – a sprig of gorse tucked into the badge.

A long-shot of the corps assembling in a clearing, carrying mess tins and cups of tea, is followed by a close-up of the Crusaders lying in long grass, their guns aimed and ready. The chaplain barks out orders, pompously, before putting a 'friendly' arm around the shoulders of a junior cadet. Tea spurts from the urn when it is hit by three bullets. The corps runs for cover and lies on the ground as gunfire – from Mick and Johnny's rifles and Wallace's sten gun – rings out. The only one standing, locked in his own fantasy world of pomp and self-service, is the chaplain, stupidly fearless. He calls the attackers out of hiding and strides over to meet them, barking out demands and orders as he goes. Mick walks forward to meet him, but stops before he gets to him. He raises and aims his rifle. The chaplain stops, starts walking again and is shot by Mick. He falls to the ground in the heather. He calls out for mercy. Mick advances, firing more rounds – blanks – and raises his bayonet. The chaplain squirms. The camera, now looking up, records Mick demonstrating the 'Yell of Hate' – the last sound he makes in the film.

A smooth cut, from the white sky as the 'Hate'-yelling Mick exits the frame to sky-white curtains, takes us inside the headmaster's office. He strides into view, looks very stern and says, 'I take this seriously.' Thus begins the most unusual scene in the film. Standing before him are Mick, Johnny and Wallace. He asks them to apologise to the chaplain. He walks over to a chest of drawers and pulls it open. The chaplain, in clerical collar, sits up. The boys file past, shake his offered hand and nod an apology. The headmaster nods for the chaplain to lie back down. Then, with his back to the chest of drawers, the headmaster closes the drawer and, as one should when one has accepted an apology and moved on, continues with the scene as though nothing strange has happened.

The scene is there because it is funny and because it makes the audience sit up and take notice (rather like the chaplain, in fact). It's a logical extension to the lunatic surrealism that has run through the film from the very first scene. It was intended to be a visual metaphor for the kind of man who keeps the Bible in the top drawer and who brings it out to give his arguments weight and 'reason'. But, because the scene is so effective, and draws so much attention to itself, I think it's a mistake. Lindsay Anderson certainly got bored with oft-repeated questions about its meaning.

As a punishment, the three boys are given the Protestant 'privilege of work'. The scene cuts to the school hall, the camera at the back of the room so that we can see much of the room. Phillips, reading a book, is sitting on the edge of a stage; before him are stacked the chairs on which parents will sit on speech day. There are piles of books and scattered furniture on the stage. A trapdoor opens. From beneath the stage, Johnny emerges in a gasmask and gets to his feet. From stage right (the camera doesn't move and the whole scene is played without cuts), Wallace hurries into the frame. He and Johnny bend down by the open trapdoor and pull from it an alligator. Phillips and Wallace carry it outside. Johnny returns back down the hole. Outside the gym, a schoolmaster supervises a bonfire, on to which the alligator is put.

I asked Lindsay whether or not the alligator was an oblique reference to *The Louisiana Story*, a favourite film of his, in which a boy stalks and tries to subdue a real alligator. In a letter to me, dated 29 June 1994, he wrote that it 'wasn't a tribute to Flaherty, I'm afraid. I wasn't thinking of *Louisiana Story*, but it's a nice idea.'

Beneath the stage, Johnny is piling up books for the bonfire; Mick finds and brings forward a stuffed eagle (symbol of America and of freedom) and hands it to Johnny, who places it down in front of an inverted wall map of the British Empire. He strokes the eagle, a gesture that suggests that, unlike the books (symbols of school), the eagle will not be added to the bonfire. He clears the way to a padlocked cupboard. Mick puts down a plaster bust he is carrying, picks up an axe and breaks the lock with a single blow. The cupboard shelves are filled with glass jars, among them a human foetus (in this context it is perhaps a symbol of the preservation of the incarceration of English children). Mick picks up the jar containing the foetus, turns around with it, and hands it to The Girl. She returns it to the shelf and closes the cupboard doors. The time is not yet right for family planning. Wallace and Phillips return to the store room beneath the stage and join the other Crusaders as they follow Mick behind the cupboard, or is it a wardrobe? Had they gone through the wardrobe they might have found the lion and the witch but, entering on their hands and knees, they find a secret room, and in the secret room, they find a chest, and in the chest, a treasure store of armaments. Fire, schoolbooks, bombs, an upturned map of the Empire. The symbols point the way to the finale. The 'house-cleaning' exercise will be carried forward to a full and proper cleaning away of the house.

CHAPTER 8: CRUSADERS

The final chapter starts with words and not pictures. Over the title card is heard a soldierly shout: 'Guard of honour … [atten]shun!' Then we see a close-up of the flag of Britain. The camera lens zooms back to set the flag in its context. It is flying from the roof of the College. The College is Anderson's symbol of Britain. A bell tolls.

More soldierly commands are shouted by Denson. A small platoon of cadets presents arms. Fronted by two motorcycle outriders, Denson's father arrives in a chauffeured car. Denson's father is General Denson, a war hero. He inspects the cadets. To the right of the cadets are three boys in surplices, Machin, Jute and Biles. Biles is carrying a large crucifix. Behind the three boys is a man in a suit of armour. Next to him is Rowntree, offering a hand of welcome. The general shakes hands with an old friend, now a bishop, another symbol of the ruling class. There's another knight in armour. Then we are inside the school hall, where a packed congregation of parents and boys are singing the school hymn. When the hymn finishes, the final verse sung by the trebles, the honoured guests have reached the stage and a strange British ceremony plays out. The headmaster kneels to kiss the ring of a knight; the two men exchange humorously nonsensical Latin phrases; the headmaster, standing, turns to the congregation and leads them in saying together: 'Gratias vobis agimus, Benefactores.'

The congregation sits. The headmaster welcomes all ranks of hierarchical society: 'Your Royal Highness, my Lord Bishop, General Denson, my lords, ladies and gentlemen ... ' He tells us that College has a quarter of the Christian era stretching behind it (not borne out by the high Victorian buildings) and, after a short speech, he introduces the main speaker, an old boy: General Denson.

Throughout the general's speech that follows, the camera picks out faces in the crowd, pleasant faces, real (as opposed to actorly) faces, parents' faces, boys' faces. In the context of what follows – the burning down of the school hall and the Crusaders' attempt to kill all these people, the young as well as the old – it's a rather curious close look at 'the enemy'; as close, in fact, as the faces of the Covent Garden porters in Anderson's elegiac documentary *Every Day Except Christmas* (1957), and the faces of the infants in *Thursday's Children* (1954). It adds a strange elegiac quality to a scene that is outrageously vicious. The key to the scene is an entry in Lindsay Anderson's diary:

> 2 January 1944: Sitting in the cadets' mess at a quarter to eleven, before a dying fire I lay down my copy of *To the Lighthouse* for I have been interrupted by Teddy Vaughan. I lay down my book and I look at him; he is young and yet he is becoming old. He is still a boy and yet there is about him an air of age, of becoming a father, of having responsibilities, of earning money and settling down. In all this there is something sad: why must youth so perish, freshness so stale, virility so harden and become coarse? He will marry and have children: it is in the nature of things. And he will become conventional and stiff. And his beauty will fade and his skin grow hard. And I am not to be persuaded that this is not a tragedy.[14]

These boys have their whole lives ahead of them, but it will be done in obedient service to the traditions that stifle their humanity and freedom.

11. *Preparing Peter Jeffrey for his final scene*

The general's speech takes the themes of 'Tradition and the Respon-
sibilities of Privilege', and the need to learn the 'habit of obedience'.
He tells the congregation that they must fight to preserve the freedoms
of class and privilege. And his rallying call backfires, literally. Smoke
rises from beneath the stage supporting not just the general but the
main guests and dignitaries. It thickens. Coughs proliferate. The school
is on fire. Amusingly, the general is so rapt by his own rhetoric that

he is the last to notice. There is applause when he announces that the traditions in the College are not going to change but, as he talks on about 'unquestioning obedience', the pupils, masters, parents and guests flee into the open air – the costumed clergy running down their fellow men – to be greeted not by words but by a mortar shell. The first to leave the hall now lie dead on the floor. The sound of machine-gun fire bursts around them, and the camera zooms in to a close-up of the assassin: Mick. On the College roof, now unloading their weapons, are Mick and The Girl, Wallace and Bobby Phillips, and Johnny. Down below, the general orders the breaking open of the armoury. The Establishment fights back. Another woman gets a speaking role. It's Machin's mother toting a machine-gun and, in an echo of the nurse's 'Fight, fight' at the rugby match, she shouts 'Bastards! Bastards!' The woman of the Establishment is passive and subservient, except when called upon to defend it. The headmaster, arms outstretched, calls for a ceasefire and is granted one until, after a rational call for reason and trust, is shot between the eyes by The Girl. He disappears in a mortar explosion. The ranks of the Establishment close in and, with the organ playing the school hymn on the soundtrack, unload their weapons on the Crusaders. The Crusaders fire back. The camera locks in a close-up of Mick's face filled with rage as he sprays down bullets. The screen goes black and silent. No title card announces 'The End'; instead, the word *'if....'* appears at the bottom right-hand corner of the screen.

The violence of the finale is as fantastical as the padre sitting up from within a chest of drawers, but it's a 'dream' or a fantasy from which there is no escape. Anderson's aim with the scene was to entertain, to puzzle, to inspire, to encourage debate. By showing the fight and the deaths of the 'innocents' (i.e. the schoolboys), he is saying that the whole (the Establishment) needs to be swept away. By focusing in on Mick he is saying that the individual will find 'freedom' not by 'unquestioning obedience' but by fighting against that very thing. There is a scowl on Mick's face, but there is also fear. The battle is going to be hard and long because the opposition is so horribly strong.

CUT SCENES

The most interesting scene that was filmed but cut from the final film was 'Matron's Dream'. This was to be placed at the moment when matron is dreaming in reverie to the sound of the flute and song serenade by the housemaster and his wife. She was dreaming of making love to a group of boys, boys running to her, boys held to her breast. There is a report from the editor David Gladwell that some of the boys were naked. Brian Pettifer was clothed when Lindsay filmed him lying on top of Mona Washbourne.[15]

Another cut scene took place in the senior dormitory on the first night:

WALLACE and FISHER facing each other. The others watch them.
WALLACE: Of course you can do it.
FISHER: Not to me you can't.
PEANUTS: It's cutting off the fresh blood to the brain that does it.
WALLACE: Ready?
FISHER: (doubtfully) No hurting ...
WALLACE puts his arms round FISHER from behind like a wrestler.
WALLACE: Breathe out – now!
As FISHER breathes out, WALLACE presses his hands into FISHER'S stomach. FISHER slumps forward unconscious. They all gather round his inert body.
PEANUTS: It's the complete lack of oxygen.
JOHNNY: He's dead.
STEPHANS: For God's sake. Get up, Fisher.
PREFECTS: (from the corridor in unison) Dormitory inspection ... now!
WALLACE and JOHNNY bundle FISHER'S body into his bed and tuck in the sheets around him. With theatrical formality the PREFECTS all troop into the senior dormitory.[16]

A scene scripted but not filmed, and which seems to lay some of the foundations for the finale of *Britannia Hospital*, took place in the science lab. This was to come after the headmaster's conference with the prefects (the 'nubile Cinderella' lecture) and before we see the juniors vaulting the gym horse:

In the middle of the laboratory a grey mass of wires, tubes and tran-sistorised circuits, about five feet high and supported on an iron frame. BOYS, and a SCIENCE MASTER, are making final adjustments to it.
SCIENCE MASTER: Right. Stand back. We will now activate the memory centres. Switch on, Machin.
Machin switches on. The machine throbs. A light runs along the wires. Other lights flash on and off at the intersections of the wires ... A

12. *Robin Askwith and friends carrying Brian Pettifer.*

brighter light zig-zags to and fro in the centre. Two heavy parallel rods on the front of the machine clonk open, like lips, and then shut.[17]

The most substantial cut scene, which featured in the headmaster's script and also in Sherwin's novelisation of the film, is a field trip to a Norman castle led, of course, by Mr Stewart. This came immediately after the caning of Travis, Johnny and Wallace, and starts with a string of boys on bicycles speeding down the lane. 'Amongst them, peddling powerfully, is Mr Stewart.' At 'Castle Cadnum', Stewart gives a long, windy lecture but abandons it because of inattention from the boys: 'Oh go on – amuse yourselves.' Pussy Graves photographs a boy lying in an open grave; Mick and Johnny wind a length of cloth round a pole and hold the ends taut; Denson and Wallace play a game with a stone, throwing it back and forth. Mick and Johnny climb the highest wall of the castle – Mick holding the pole between his teeth. On top of the battlements, they let their 'flag' unfold and they take in the all-round view. Intercut with shots of Mick and Johnny in close-up, there follows a series of long-shots of Britain: the Wiltshire Downs, an industrial city, a street scene, Snowdonia, the Cornish coast, the sea, the Royal Lancaster Hotel, a railway train crossing the Forth Bridge, Blenheim Palace, a power station.

After this, we are back at College. In the dining hall, Rowntree announces that College House has won the College marathon race.[18]

THREE
The Reception, the Sequel

THE CENSORS

Unlike his predecessors, and many of the men and women who have since scissored in on the censor's office, the British censor, John Trevelyan, was neither puritan nor philistine. To ease the film's passage past the censor's board (of which Lord Harlech was chairman), Lindsay corresponded with Trevelyan while the film was in production. On 1 July 1968, Trevelyan wrote to Lindsay about seven points of possible concern:

> 1. The bullying of Biles in the lavatories. I think that, taking into account what the film is saying, this would not be likely to be regarded as gratuitous sadism.
> 2. The phrase 'dirty little bugger' would probably pass in a film of this kind.
> 3. You might be asked to remove to shots of boys naked in the shower-bath.
> 4. I think that you would almost certainly be asked to remove the fantasy shot of Travis and the girl naked together on the floor of the cafe, so I think that you would be wise either to trim it now to an absolute minimum or to remove it before the film comes in for censorship.
> 5. I think that the beating scene would probably be accepted in the context of the film's message; in another kind of film it might be regarded as excessively sadistic.
> 6. I think that a note would be made of the shot of Wallace and the young blond boy in bed together, but since they are both sleeping it might possibly pass.
> 7. I think you would certainly be asked to remove the front-view shot of Mrs Kemp walking naked down the corridor; the subsequent back view shots of her in the dormitory would probably pass.[1]

Lindsay trimmed the cafe scene to an absolute minimum (it was accidentally screened uncut when the film was first shown on British television); Gary Ross's sweeping removal of his towel in front of the camera, and frontal shots of the showering boys, were replaced with a more modest alternative take.

'The front-view shot of Mrs Kemp does present us with a real problem,' wrote Trevelyan to Anderson on 27 August 1968, 'if only because I raised this particular issue only a few months ago, and to accept a shot like this now could put us in an embarrassing position. However, I will see what it looks like before making any further comment ... The same will presumably apply to the changing-room scene if this remains as before.'[2]

Mrs Kemp was allowed to wander naked through the school, but this was trimmed to keep her frontal nudity at a distance. In America, the British-release cut of the film was rated 'X' but passed without further cuts, though this 'uncut' version played only in New York City. For national distribution, the nude scenes were cut and the film rerated 'A'. Australia cut the film even for its première at the Sydney Film Festival (where puritan zealots within the police force would disgrace themselves in 2002 by pulling a print of Larry Clark's *Ken Park* from the projector). Italy banned the film until the ban was overturned after vigorous protests in the press. In South Africa, the film was banned to black people and heavily censored for 'white-only' screenings. The sixteen South African censor cuts included Wallace licking the picture in the magazine, 'all dialogue referring to sex', and the shot of Wallace and Phillips in bed together.[3]

The cut 'A'-rated American version of the film was beautifully restored for a 2002 British theatrical rerelease. The most complete print in circulation is one that screens regularly on German TV, but that is missing the Brechtian titles.

PARAMOUNT

There were supporters within Paramount who liked the film and who stuck with it, but there was concern at executive level. Terence Feely of Paramount UK wrote to Lindsay on 6 September 1968:

Despite my increasing sympathy with the picture and my growing identification – through repeated exposure – with it, there are some points to which people who saw it for the first time today have drawn to my attention ... The fantasies and the lack of any help in recognising them have again been repeatedly mentioned. The music does not give a cue as we hoped it would and people have been groping for guidance to know where they are. The confusion seems to start in the fight between Michael and the girl at the cafe. I am sure it would help if the flash of them fighting naked were to be preceded by a shot of Johnnie watching them so that at least we could assume that this is his fantasy.

The other point which I found was universally commented on was that of the padre in the drawer. If we could lose that particular shot and somehow convey that the shooting and bayoneting of the padre was again a fantasy of Mick's I am sure this would go a long way towards relieving confusion.

Is there nothing more you can do to accommodate us on these points? What happened to your idea of a musical cue to each of the fantasy sequences?[4]

There was nothing that Lindsay could do to accommodate them on those points. In America, Paramount tried and failed to sell the film to an art-house chain. In Britain, it was saved from oblivion by a ruling by the Eady quota, an innovation introduced by Harold Wilson when he was at the Board of Trade in the Clement Attlee government, that stipulated that a certain number of films shown in British cinemas had to be British. In December 1968, *Barbarella* was pulled after two unsuccessful weeks at the Paramount cinema in the West End, and *if....* was put on in its place.

The film was an immediate box-office success. A circuit release was arranged for the spring. In an interview with Jules Cohen, published in *Pangolin* in February 1970, Lindsay said:

We can all too easily get in the habit of moaning about distributors. There's a lot to moan about. I would say, from my own position at the moment, being absolutely objective, that in fact I think Paramount has behaved very well and very intelligently in relation to *if....*, and I hope this will set a precedent for the handling of this type of picture. They're doing their best for it.

CHELTENHAM AND ALDENHAM

'Lindsay Conned Us All' screamed the banner headline in the College newspaper, beneath which the headmaster, David Ashcroft, explained why he was going back on his decision to screen the film in school:

There were several important departures from the synopsis. The most important, a scene which becomes central to the film, is the beating of the three recalcitrants by the head of house in the gym: in the synopsis they were to be lectured to for mobbing about and being unco-operative and given a minor cautionary punishment. The beating is a protracted scene and the camera dwells almost lovingly on the brutality and pain. There are other similar additions, not in the original, all putting the emphasis on calculated brutality, one a horrid scene in the lavatories, another after the field-day tea-scene, when the chaplain gets shot and the camera lingers on him as he writhes on the ground being threatened by the boy who clubs him with the rifle. There are also prurient suggestions of homosexuality, which are unrelated to the theme and seem to me to be a cheap deference to the box-office ... You will obviously want to see it because of your involvement and many of you appear very photogenic; I shall be interested in your reactions, but I am not now inclined to take steps to have it specially shown here.[5]

A lively debate was carried out on the letters page of the local newspaper: 'Sir,' snorted Irene Houghton-Ridley (Mrs), an indignant resident of Montpellier Grove, 'I quite agree with "Resident's" remarks in his letter headed 'Utterly Boring' – I too feel ashamed that such a fine school as Cheltenham College should be chosen for such an extraordinary, disgusting, and incredible film.' An anonymous letter signed merely 'Shocked' wrote that 'The fantasy was adolescent, and for me the entire film spoke only of immaturity. If I've missed the point I beg to be excused. I did enjoy the scenery, though – fit for young and old. Such unabashed views of 'old Cheltenham' and the washroom ... Oh my!!' But not all the letters were from lunatics. A. D. Grant wrote that 'It may represent the public school of long ago, but hasn't the system now been extended to our whole world? Rigid organisation, cramped living, pointless rules, petty tyrannies, unjust punishments; we are all grumbling against these and a hundred other horrors paralleled in the film.' Stephen Davies wrote in to say:

I, my wife and colleagues at work found it stimulating, at times extremely funny, and at others most moving and almost frightening in its portrayal of the impact upon young boys of suddenly finding themselves in a tough, cruel and utterly masculine environment. There certainly were interludes of fantasy, but these seemed to spring naturally from the experience and conversations of the rebel trio whose progress we were following.[6]

13. *Malcolm McDowell as Mick Travis eyeing up BSA motorbikes*

Paul Griffin, the headmaster of Aldenham School, liked the film more than his equivalent at Cheltenham: 'In truth it is a brilliant film', but in his letter to Anderson, on 17 January 1969, he felt he had much to complain about:

> You said before you started here that you had no intention of attacking the public schools. The trouble is that in basing a study of decayed authority on the public schools, you have been able to convey such truth in detail that the whole argument seems particularised. At a time when he we are struggling against a bad image, I think you have done us quite a lot of harm; even while serving the cinema well.

Incredibly – and a clearer image of the ivory tower mentality cannot be found – Griffin went on to complain that Aldenham could be recognised publicly because of two portraits seen in the film:

> Your use of the portrait of our founder, Richard Platt, and that of my predecessor, Dr Cooke. In the first case, I think it quite wrong to use the picture of a real person to brood over your imaginary school. It upsets people who have been brought up with the portrait, and it

identifies Aldenham. In Dr Cooke's case, we have a man beloved by numbers of people still living who do not fancy this association. My permission for you to use the buildings surely cannot have implied the right to use these portraits.[7]

Was the film fair? Were the public schools institutions of privilege staffed by half-mad savages?

From information provided from *Public Schools Commission. First Report* (Vol. 1) and from the book *The Public Schools: A Factual Survey* by Graham Kalton, one learns the following facts.

Of all the children who left school in 1966, only five in every two hundred came from public schools. Yet they took one of every three places at Oxford and Cambridge, and over 15 per cent of all the university places available. In January 1964 about three out every five male teachers in all secondary or 'government' schools had no degree. In grammar schools (government-financed) about one in five male teachers had no degree. In public schools, seven out of every eight were graduates. In 1966 more than 90 per cent of the Conservative cabinet were from public schools; as were more than 40 per cent of the Labour cabinet which succeeded them. Between 1963 and 1967 ex-public school boys provided almost half the recruits for the administrative class of the Civil Service, and about 60 per cent for the Diplomatic Service.

In 1967 ex-public school boys accounted for 55 per cent of admirals, generals and air chief marshals, and more than 65 per cent of physicians and surgeons in the General Medical Council. Seventy per cent of directors of prominent firms, 75 per cent of Church of England bishops; and about 80 per cent of judges and QCs came up from the 'five in every two hundred citizens' who went to a public school.

In the five schools with the highest fees as many of 55 per cent of new boys were the sons of men who had been to that same school.

In the school year 1962–63, three out of every five independent boarding schools had a system of 'fagging': younger boys obliged to do chores and 'services' for older boys. In ninety-one out of ninety-eight such schools, masters other than the headmaster and his deputy were allowed to cane or 'whip' the boys. In seventy-one of these, pupils also had the power to whip other boys. In eleven of these, this 'privilege' was restricted to the head boy. In six schools more than fifty boys had the power and 'privilege' to administer corporal punishment.

In twelve boarding schools the number of canings by masters exceeded a hundred a year. In four schools it exceeded three hundred and fifty a year. In one school the number of beatings by masters and boys averaged more than two beatings per pupil per year.

I personally attended a school where one very inadequate teacher regularly took pleasure and pride in caning the whole class if one person didn't hear his command to 'be quiet'.

FELLOW ARTISTS AND FAMOUS FANS

After completing the film, Lindsay wrote to most of the boys listed in the cast and gave them a gift of a book, usually Karen Blixen's *Out of Africa*. Some of the boys' replies are kept in the Lindsay Anderson Archive at Stirling University. 'Thanks very much for the your letter, for the book – which I've much enjoyed reading – and the advice and warnings, which of course I appreciate. And thank you for giving me the part in *if*...., which was a fantastic experience,' wrote Hugh Thomas (Denson) from Merton College, Oxford, adding that 'an elderly lady came up and said she was a mistress in a girls' school, and the film had made her think that she had wasted twenty years teaching! It was really rather sad – the poor lady was quite obviously shattered by it' (11 January 1969).

Sean Bury (Jute): 'Thank you very much indeed for the book and also for your kind letter ... My mother sends her regards; she is now feeding our various pets ... excluding me.'

Richard Everett (Pussy Graves) wrote that the film 'must surely be one of the greatest of its kind ... at the end [of the screening he attended] there was complete astonishment' (6 December 1968).

Robert Swann (Rowntree): 'People keep stopping me – in pubs and sometimes in the streets to say how much they have enjoyed *if*..... It was very exciting to see the queues stretching round the block ... I've only just begun to read *Out of Africa*, only the first chapter but I can see why you sent it to me.'

Guy Ross (Stephans): 'Just thought I would write to thank you for everything that was so fantastic about working with you. It's so rare to feel such admiration for one's director' (undated).

Brian Pettifer (Biles): 'Enclosed are two photographs of yourself, sincerely hope you like them. The others I took were unfortunately in the camera which was stolen ... Hope to meet you again Lindsay.'

One of the most welcome 'fan' letters was from Akira Kurosawa, whom Lindsay probably first met at the opening of the National Film Theatre on the South Bank in 1957. Kurosawa saw the film at Cannes,

14. *Geoffrey Chater telling Guy Ross to fight temptation.*

and wrote expressing his 'heartfelt congratulations on winning the Grand Prix ... I would like to apologise for my long silence ... I should be very happy if I could have a chance to meet you in the near future and resume our old acquaintance' (16 June 1969).

'You're right – you're right – you're right. That is the system that you and I have been put through,' wrote actor James Fox, 'and that is what my young brother Robert is going through at the moment at Harrow, because my family have been brain-washed by the "system" into sending their son to the same place, despite its educationally and emotionally harmful effects on Edward and myself ... There is no exaggeration in *if....* ' (undated).

Richard Lester wrote to thank Lindsay 'for making such a powerful, intelligent, and entertaining film. I think it is a great benefit to all of us who make films to see that beautifully cast, acted, photographed and planned films can be made within the clutches of commercial cinema' (23 December 1968).

John Boorman declared the film to be 'stunning and brilliant ... Would love to have the chance to talk to you about it, and to see it a few more times' (undated).

Rex Harrison, whom Lindsay would direct on Broadway in a 1981 production of *The Kingfisher*, wrote: 'I do admire you, how anybody with such a fire in the belly can be so convivial, both in your work and in yourself. There was no one untrue performance, thanks to you. You are right, it is a film for the youth of today. They will eat it up, as we did.'

From the theatrical world, Harold Pinter called it 'a magnificent fucking film ... proudest congratulations and a warm embrace. You've really done something!' (15 January 1969).

Bernard Miles wrote that 'it's truly great, a very deep look not only at school life but at what we venture to call civilisation and the human situation in general!'

Michael Croft 'admired the film and was moved by it ... I once taught at Cheltenham 18 years ago – not the college but the junior school over the road which was worse – the most miserable three months of my life. My only happy memory is of the rugger match between the college and Gloucester when I picked up the ball which had gone out of touch and booted it with great force and quite unintentionally straight up the arse of the headmaster who was sitting on his shooting stick 20 yards away' (19 December 1969).

The poet, John Betjeman, wrote several times: 'Dear and great director, White, frail and gentle Elizabeth Cavendish told me you never got my first fan letter after seeing *if*.... Well here is my second. It seemed to me a faultless film ... I was able to identify myself with the hero. But I never had his guts. Sound, characterisation, humour, agony and colour subtlety and beauty of the shots (and my word, wasn't the tart good!)' (10 September 1969).

David Cornwell (John Le Carré) wrote: 'I saw *if*.... Superbly delicate casting, beautiful and sad film, lovely rhythm. No buts. Just a marvellous film' (15 May 1969).

Alan Bennett: 'I saw *if*.... today and herewith eat my words. I enjoyed it enormously ... though I don't agree with lots of it. Particularly I liked Biles and Graham Crowden in the classroom' (undated).

The only dissenting voice was from Vanessa Redgrave: 'I didn't come to see you after *if*.... because I didn't want to tell polite things and I didn't want to say depressingly that I didn't really like it ... I was perhaps disappointed that the hero's outbreaks were all fantasy ... It's strange but I kept also thinking of the man in America who took a shotgun and killed all those people from the top of the tower' (undated).

Vanessa Redgrave wasn't suggesting that the film was an incitement to violence, but was it? Students at Harrow, the public school which counted twenty-seven prime ministers among its alumni, were inspired to form a branch of the Revolutionary Schools Action Union. National newspapers in England reported, on 22 June 1969, that more than thirty boys at Harrow School had been expelled, asked to leave, or rusticated in a crackdown on the group of rebels who had been defying the school's strict discipline. The *Telegraph* reporter recorded that: 'Another boy ran up to tell me they wanted to abolish distinctions between pupils. He said it was disgraceful they should be beaten by older boys. Lindsay Anderson gave an exceptionally good picture of what public schools are like. Much of the film can be traced to Harrow.'

Lindsay Anderson had guessed (hoped?) that such actions would be forthcoming. In his self-interview he asked the question: 'Do you think that the film's attitude towards all this could be taken as an incitement to violence?

A: I can't see why it should. The work is not a propagandist one. It doesn't preach. It never makes any kind of explicit case. It gives you a situation and shows what happens in this particular instance when certain forces on the one side are set against certain forces on the other, without any mutual understanding. The aim of the picture is not to incite but to help people to understand the resulting conflict.[8]

In 2003, another film about another school massacre won the Palme d'Or at Cannes. Like Lindsay Anderson's film before it, Gus Van Sant's *Elephant* is a portrait of a school, the school serving as a metaphor for society, which ends with pupils machine-gunning away the staff and their fellow pupils. Gus Van Sant's film was inspired not by *if....* but by the real-life tragedy at the Columbine High School, USA, where on 20 April 1999 twelve pupils and a teacher were killed by boys armed with bombs and guns. There is no evidence to suggest that the Columbine killers were inspired by, or had ever seen, *if.....* The similarities between *if....* and *Elephant* are only skin-deep and the essential differences profound. The killings in *if....* are clearly metaphorical and, unlike the killers in Elephant, Mick Travis in *if....* is not deranged, he's a hero. When talking about his film, Anderson liked to use the word 'healthy' and he insisted that Mick was:

an old-fashioned hero. He's well-balanced, got a sense of humour, absolutely healthy. All his instincts are good and correct. He has a strong feeling for proper human relationships as opposed to the false and phony human relationships which are cultivated by the system he ends up rebelling against. His friendship with the three boys is a very good, friendly, felt relationship. You compare the scene when you see the whips all talking together in this terrible snide sort of way – preoccupied with phony ideas of tradition; or the others, with this sort of terrible camp gossip about the little boys, and then you see the other three boys in the study – it's a great difference between them.[9]

BRITISH CRITICS

Perhaps the first major British press notice was written by the *Guardian*'s Derek Malcolm, summing up the last week of the 1968 London Film Festival. After writing about Godard's *One Plus One*, Truffaut's *Les Baisers Volés*, Wajda's *Everything for Sale* and Ingmar Bergman's *Shame*, he wrote:

If Lindsay Anderson's *if....* gets shown abroad ... it should do much to prove there's hope for the British yet. Not only in the matter of making technically first-class films, but also as far as content is concerned. This is light years ahead of the nerveless twists of Boultingland ... The mixture of realism, parody, poetry and fantasy grows uncomfortable at times. But at least it's full-bloodedly alive, vividly imagined, beautifully acted and true to itself throughout. And of how many British films can one say all that?[10]

The press show for the British release was held at the Paramount Theatre, Piccadilly Circus on 17 December at 10.30 a.m. It was released in London and reviewed in the same week as *Chitty Chitty Bang Bang* and took all the headlines. In the *Observer*, Penelope Mortimer started with a witty wink to Kipling: 'If .... you can make a film opposed to all commercial concepts, and make a success of it, you very probably have a touch of genius, my son' and added that 'Lindsay Anderson's handling of the subject is masterly ... The performances excel anything I have seen on the screen for a very long time.'[11]

Dilys Powell, in the *Sunday Times*, called it 'a splendid first-hand film ... all the fragments merge to make cinema, a true film'.[12]

Patrick Gibbs, in the *Daily Telegraph*, noted that *if*.... was 'an inventive and well-organised satire: indeed, the film as a whole is superbly executed, script, actors and scene being handled with much technical skill and style. Only the setting I find questionable. Had this been a contemporary university with a reactionary staff and rigid system being ridiculed, then the satire might well have found its mark.' Gibbs claimed that it had all been done before and listed a fetishist's collection:

> Lytton Strachey's portrait of Arnold of Rugby written just 50 years ago, though H. A. Vachell's novel *The Hill*, based on Harrow, was a pioneer in its treatment of adolescent homosexuality. Since then the fire has been continuous and withering ... Most recently we have had David Benedictus taking it out of Eton in *The Fourth of June* and Cuthbert Worsley's *Flannelled Fool*, with its hair-raising memories of public school as master and boy. And isn't Alan Bennett now poking fun at the system every night in his play *Forty Years On?*.

But Gibbs did like the 'allusions to homosexual relations, which are handled with a beautifully sure and light touch. Such love, it is suggested, is the only fine feature in this brutish world.'[13]

'One certainly knew that Mr Anderson had *if*.... in him, and out of him', wrote John Coleman in the *New Statesman*.

> He has always been a startlingly sympathetic director of actors and non-actors and here excels himself ... [but] I cannot regard *if*.... as a complex comment on the end of civilisation as we know it, notwithstanding those student riots and all. Mr Anderson remains more of an impatient aristocrat in his dealings with humanity in the everyday sense than some of his public pronouncements might lead the unwary to believe.

He didn't like 'at least two jokes which totally misfired ... the housemaster and his wife sitting up in their twin beds, he warbling to her recorder, and the surreal business of the chaplain being pulled out of a drawer', but added that Anderson 'is closer to Buñuel in his iconoclasm, and the closer he subsequently gets to that master the better his work will be'.[14]

Coleman was banned by Anderson from attending his 1977 National Film Theatre retrospective.

David Wilson, in the *Monthly Film Bulletin* wrote:

> *if*.... is neither a prophecy nor a call to arms; it is rather a disturbingly

accurate analysis of a society whose art (for instance) responds with the despair of Francis Bacon or the wistful escapism of David Hockney and *Yellow Submarine*. The school may be imaginary, but what happens behind those Victorian Gothic walls is only too real. David Sherwin's script sketches in the details with masterful economy.[15]

AMERICAN CRITICS

The film opened in America in March 1969. Joseph Gelmis, who would interview Lindsay Anderson at length in the book *The Director as Superstar* (1970) called the film 'a masterpiece which transcends distinctions of realism or fantasy and establishes its own unique form and style'.[16] Richard Schickel in *Life* wrote:

We have been smoothly but forcibly transported from our traditional position of coolly objective observers of human behavior into experiencing what it is like to live again inside the skin of an adolescent. One is reminded how very sweaty and feverish it is in there, difficult to breathe because the space is crowded with dusty cartons of conventional wisdom left there by careless adults and the fantasy a kid manufactures for himself out of misapprehension and undischarged imaginative energy.[17]

'The history of College goes back to the Crusades,' wrote Robert Kotlowitz in a fine reading of the film in *Harper's* magazine.

It is a period in time for which the school's toothy officials feel an incontrollable nostalgia. For them, all good things stem from those barbaric journeys eastward, made in the name of God: honor, dignity, purpose, courage, moral energy, and the sense of serving the nation that assures a man that he is an Englishman and not a member of some lesser breed.

When the school seems to lose its idea of itself and the students have forgotten what it means to cheer its athletic teams on to victory, the administration holds a kind of founders' day celebration. The theme is Crusaders' Spirit. Stouthearted generals from the Second World War – old boys from College – speak to the young generation with a toothpaste-ad cheer and the kind of blind composure that once could plan and carry out, for example, the slaughter on the Somme, then justify it ... Meanwhile the ushers who serve on founders' day wear knights' armor and the insignia of the saviors of Jerusalem. The school chaplain, on the other hand, whose chief pleasures are leading army maneuvers in which College takes part and listening to confessions of sexual guilt from suffering students, is clothed in the red-gold robes of a bishop eager to take hold of his Saracen dominions. It is all shadow play, a false and inflated Halloween indulgence for adults ... Of course, no contemporary adolescent should be able to maintain his self respect in such a place.[18]

Albert Johnson, in the journal *Film Quarterly*, started his review with:

If there had ever been any doubt that Lindsay Anderson's second feature would surpass any of the recent films made in Great Britain, or that after all these years, the imagination and compassion for humanity exhibited in *This Sporting Life* (1963) would finally find a cinematic outlet again, then the time has come for suspension of doubt and acknowledgement of his genius.[19]

THE PUBLIC

RUPERT WEBSTER (Bobby Phillips): I did get fan-mail. I was at public school when I got this letter from a girl in Japan. She sent a picture of herself and return postage and a wonderful amorous letter. I was fourteen years old. I was about to write back when, the next day, I got about twenty more letters from Japanese girls. I thought if I wrote to one I would have to write to all of them. The next day I got a hundred letters, then hundreds and hundreds forwarded from the distribution company. I was tempted to write to them but I had homework to do. I feel bad about it now but it was too much. I was swamped and I didn't have a secretary. I was big in Japan, perhaps it was the floppy hair.[20]

Webster's face was prominent on the Japanese film poster.

Eighty-six prints were struck for the film's American release; 197 for Britain and the rest of the world. The film was a box-office success, particularly in New York City, where the uncut film grossed more money than it did in the whole of Great Britain. By 25 December 1971, Paramount had received the following returns from theatre owners (minus their cut): New York – $477,994, Chicago – $162,585, San Francisco – $153,482, USA total – $1,716,735, UK – $469,013, France – $429,287, Germany – $163,146, Japan – $141,002.[21] To get an approximation of how much this would be at current prices, times the figure by eighty.

By 22 December 1979, the film had made a net profit of $1,000,331, of
which Lindsay Anderson's net share was $187,804.

The film remained in circulation, screening on campus and reper-
tory cinemas throughout America and Europe. By 28 January 1984,
the money received by Paramount included: USA – $2,140,706.61,
GB – $541,936.50, France – $418,951, Italy – $167,408.50

O LUCKY MAN! AND *IF(2)*....

MALCOLM MCDOWELL: At Cannes, I said to Lindsay, we are obviously
a very successful duo, why don't we make another film together? His
eyes rolled. He said, 'Malcolm, where do you think good scripts come
from? Do you think they fall out of the trees like the leaves? If you
want to make another film with me, you'd better write it.[22]

Malcolm McDowell wrote a forty-page treatment called 'Coffee
Man', inspired by his adventures as a coffee salesman. With David Sherwin he expanded it to feature length. This fused with a documentary idea
that Lindsay was working on with Alan Price, and metamorphosed into
a *Candide*-like adventure that spanned the length of Britain to become
O Lucky Man!, still the best British film ever made. All the adult actors
from *if*.... returned in multiple roles. Ondricek was the cinematographer;
Jocelyn Herbert designed the production. The Mick Travis trilogy
started by *if*.... was completed by *Britannia Hospital* (1982), but neither
this nor *O Lucky Man!* was a sequel to *if*..... Anderson and Sherwin were
working on *if(2)*.... at the time of Anderson's death in 1994. Paramount
commissioned a script. Permission was granted to film at Cheltenham
College. A first draft was completed in February 1994.

The film opens with a repeat of the final scene from *if*...., from the
procession to the burning of the school and the close-up of Mick firing
from the roof of the chapel. Blackout. Title card – 'Today'. A train
emerges from a tunnel. Inside the train, Major Wallace, minus an arm,
looks out on different landscapes of Britain. We see a dead swan lying
across power lines. Also inside the train are four old boys, including
Jute. They talk about Wallace getting expelled and the fact that there
are now girls at College. Wallace arrives at College in a cab. At the
College, a girl, practising a reading in the chapel is being tutored by
Mrs Thomas, who tells Wallace that he and his friends are known to
her through her husband, now the housemaster of College House.
Johnny, now a clergyman in clerical collar and jeans, returns to College

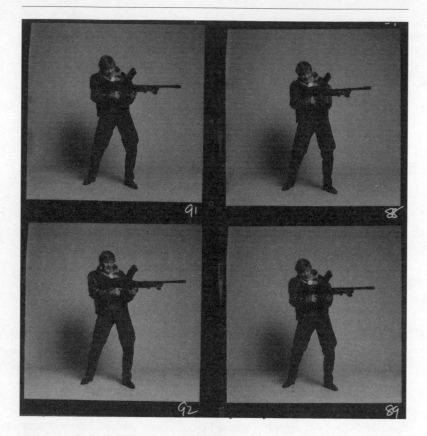

15. *Malcolm McDowell wardrobe shots for the final scene*

House, squeezing his decrepit mini in a space between a Jaguar and a BMW. A boy takes his bags and welcomes him to the Founders' Day celebrations. He walks around the school and visits the Sweat Room, now the Common Room, unisex, furnished with comfortable chairs. Inside, pupils compete in a video game contest. Fagging and scumming are no more. Johnny enters the gym and remembers Mick being caned by Rowntree and, back in the present, meets Wallace. In the space that used to be their old studies they find two students working on an architectural project: a working-class estate for 7,000 families, with separate areas for Asians and Blacks.

The housemaster hosts tea for co-Heads of the House, Sarah Rowntree and Paul Moi (from Kenya) and a large party of distinguished old boys and old girls. Johnny and Wallace enter during John Thomas's welcome speech in which he points out several old faces, including Biles, now a hospital administrator. He also explains the sleeping arrangements. Old boys and husbands in the College library, old girls and wives in the College museum. Handing out sandwiches, Sarah introduces herself to Wallace and Johnny. 'I expect you knew my father ... Will Mick Travis be coming?' Her father, now the Minister of War, is the guest of honour tomorrow, when he will make a speech and lay the foundation stone for a new College House. Johnny and Wallace discreetly evade the reunion photograph. On the sports field they see girls practising cricket. Later, they climb on to the College roof, talk about Mick and 'that amazing girl' and conclude that it is unlikely Mick will come because, 'He's a Hollywood star. Why should he want to come? He loves America. He can't stand England.' Wallace remembers Bobby Phillips, confesses that they did love each other and that Phillips became a criminal lawyer in New York. When the College clock chimes half-past six, the sound of music on a tape recorder plays. It is the Sanctus from the *Missa Luba*. Lying against the sloping tiles is Mick Travis. He springs to his feet and switches the recorder off. He's staying in his Winnebago with his wife, Sammy. He tells of getting a job as a coffee salesman, which led, via a chance audition, to a career as a Hollywood star. 'I've got a première next week in Leicester Square ... I've got to be presented to Her Royal Highness Something or other ... I once really did believe all that stuff about humanity – the indestructible human spirit – up here, blazing away at the whole silly, stupid hypocritical lot down there ... I see things differently now. Work – success – looking after my family – they're the only things that matter now.'

He takes Wallace and Johnny to meet his wife and see the mobile home. His wife plays the videotape of *Caligula*. Mick repeats the dance he did in the film. Outside, the dinner party is interrupted by the roar of a motorbike. It is Keating. On the back of the bike is Carmen, a pop singer, 'number two in the charts', who is singing at the dance tomorrow. Carmen asks to be taken to the ammunition store beneath the school stage. On the way, they hide when a master and a boy pass them. The boy is called Anderson and is told by the master, 'You know Anderson, if you go on like this, you're going to be *persona non grata* with a great many people.' The boy replies: 'You're probably right, sir, but it's too late to change.'

Carmen uses a hair-clip to open the locked hall door. The group enter the store room through the trapdoor on the stage (a flashback to the foetus). The cellar beyond the cupboard is empty, but voices can be heard. Light comes from a tunnel. In what was once the boiler room, five boys and girls (including Paul Moi) are plotting to disrupt the dance and kidnap Rowntree. Unseen, Mick and the group listen to the complete plan, which now evolves into a plan not only to kidnap Rowntree but to kill him, Paul saying, 'If we make a statement, the media will rubbish us they way they do every dissenting action. Our action will speak for itself.' Carmen interrupts the meeting. She is followed by Mick and company. The new Crusaders recognise the old 'as friends'. Mick warns about underestimating the opposition. 'That was our mistake. Learn from us.'

The following day, preparations for the College dance are going well. The headmaster, the same man from *if*...., is shadowed by Dr Kim, headmaster of Thatcher Academy in Ho-Chi Minh City (they'll be swapping jobs in the next academic term). The head is delighted that Alan Price will be playing at the dance.

Breakfast for the old boys, during which Biles's request for a second omelette is turned down ('Sorry sir – only one apiece'), is followed by a breakfast scene in Mick's camper van for Wallace, Johnny, Keating and Sammy, who finds College fascinating. Mick says he is going to visit 'Christine', still working at the Packhorse Cafe.

The headmaster gives a speech to the Founders' Day attendees in which he lists the achievements of the imperialist past and present – 'last year saw our first production of Sir Andrew Lloyd-Webber's *Cats* in the new Sir Anthony Hopkins Theatre'. All sing the College hymn.

Mr Stewart is talking to a class about 'Europe in the twentieth century and the failure of Revolution'. His question – 'Bliss was it that dawn to be alive, but to be young was very Heaven ... Which poet and which successful revolution?' is answered correctly by Mick Travis, who now enters the classroom. Stewart introduces him to the class as a film star: 'He once sat where you are sitting now.' With the class set to work on a twenty-minute essay, Stewart tells Mick that he is retiring at the end of the term and will bicycle around the world: 'Of course they may find me dead in the Gobi Desert.'

In woodlands, the new Crusaders are making their preparations.

Johnny visits Mrs Kemp in hospital. She is dying from cancer. She says she admired his rooftop assault on Founders' Day: 'You fought a good fight. That's what matters.'

On the motorbike borrowed from Keating, Mick goes to the Packhorse Cafe and meets Christine, now Mrs Roche, the manageress. She says of their adventure: 'That was a real lark! I still laugh about it.' She declines his invitation to go to the dance with him. A shoplifter is rugby-tackled by 'a huge black woman' and Christine's two teenage sons arrive and ask for money to hire a video cassette.

Keating and Wallace star in the Founders' Day cricket match against the College XI. One-armed Wallace steps in to hit the six that wins the game when the first-choice batsman suffers heatstroke.

Evening. The Marquee. Alan Price and Carmen perform for the old boys and old girls of College. The headmaster introduces Sir Robin Rowntree and, unexpectedly, Mick Travis, 'twice nominated for an Oscar'. With the spotlight on him, Mick is ushered forward to 'come and say hullo to your old friend'. As he stands face to face with Rowntree, and shakes his hand, there are flashbacks to the pre-caning and the caning scene from *if.....*

Rowntree gives a speech on the theme of 'pride'. Alan Price gets everybody dancing. Rowntree is ushered out of the tent by one of the new Crusaders: 'A phone message for you, sir, from Downing Street.'

Outside, Rowntree is rendered unconscious and carried across the field to the road. Mick's wife, Sammy, who saw them leave, tells Mick, who then follows suit. Mick confronts the abductors: 'Stop that! For God's sake think!'. But Rowntree is driven away. Mick, Wallace, Johnny, Sammy and Rowntree's daughter (also chloroformed in the kidnapping) follow in Mick's Winnebago. Keating and Carmen go ahead on Keating's motorbike.

A flashback to a shack in the woods being attacked by schoolboys playing soldiers takes us to where Rowntree is being held. Conscious, but bound, he threatens his captors. They cover his mouth with tape and he is told by Paul, the co-head boy, that: 'We're doing this to make people aware of what is being done in their names. Done by people like you. The world is being destroyed. By war and by waste ... Leaders like you make Al Capone look like Mother Teresa.'

Mick and company arrive at the hut. Mick crashes through the door: 'What do you think you're doing? Are you all mad? ... You won't stop a single war by killing a man like him. All you'll do is turn him into a martyr.' He pulls the gag from Rowntree's face. Rowntree thanks him and makes a speech about why he should not be ashamed to be rich and to be a leader and addresses Mick as a brother: 'We're on the same side! We're brothers!'

Mick takes hold of a large nail and hammer, positions the nail on Rowntree's palm, and crucifies him.

The scene cuts to the royal charity première of the film *if(2)*....
Crowds throng the pavement. A red carpet leads to the foyer. The
crew are in line to meet a member of the royal family. She arrives in
a black Rolls-Royce flanked by motorcycle out-riders. Rowntree, his
hand bandaged and in a sling, steps forward to receive her. The princess
works her way down the presentation line. She comes to Mick. Rowntree
gestures and a flunkey steps forward holding a silver tray. On the tray
is a gun. The princess hands the gun to Mick, who bows and takes it
from her. He steps forward and adopts the firing position. Everyone
applauds. He takes a different position, aggressively.[23]

FOUR
Conclusion

In 1993, in the year before he died, Lindsay Anderson gave the Edinburgh Film Festival lecture:

> When I was invited to give this address I was rather flattered, then rather intimidated, then I thought I should accept. Then I realised that the time was a bit short – obviously someone had dropped out. Who, I wondered, could this be? I was told, Martin Scorsese. Ah yes, I said, of course. For Martin Scorsese, besides being one of the most famous as well as one of the most successful directors in the world today, is also an American. And I realised that if any film-maker was going to be invited to make a speech at a British film festival today, he would have to be an American. For the Americans – as anyone who tries to make a British picture today will soon find out – have certainly won: artistically, financially and in their effortless domination of the media ... So when I heard that I would be replacing Martin Scorsese at Edinburgh, I knew that I would have to apologise – for not being American ... I'm sorry I haven't time to deplore the present triumph of the media – and the surrender of the media to the values of Hollywood: the Oscars; the American faces on the cover of the *Radio Times*; the vital importance of American names. Let me remind you that not a single one of those British renaissance films [made by Tony Richardson, Karel Reisz and myself] featured an American. Today Tom Jones would have to be played by Tom Cruise. I wanted to finish this address with the last sequence of *if....* and to ask you with whom you identify. But no print of *if....* is available from the National Film Archive. Need I say more?[1]

if.... succeeded in the global markets not by pandering to 'American' taste, which is the way of film-making in Britain today, but by assimilating the best that world cinema and the world film heritage could offer, then being true to itself, i.e. being uniquely British. Anderson's 'no compromise' approach to film-making, picked up from Milos Forman in Czechoslovakia, Andrzej Wajda in Poland and Satyajit Ray in India, meant that he was able to make very few films in Britain, where compromise is seen as a way of life. Between *O Lucky Man!*, released in 1973, and *Britannia Hospital*, released in 1982, Lindsay Anderson made only one more full-length film work: *The Old Crowd* for Thames Television.[2] Adapted by Anderson and Alan Bennett from a story by Alan Bennett, and amazingly filmed in three days, *The Old Crowd* takes a bourgeois couple's housewarming dinner party as its starting point, builds on the epic non-naturalistic structure of *if....*, features great performances by Rachel Roberts, Jill Bennett and Valentine Dyall (making perhaps the finest entrance in film history) and was met with such a howl of protest on its broadcast in 1979 that Bennett and producer, Stephen Frears, were summoned on to the 'South Bank Show' to apologise for it. Apologise they did not. Lindsay Anderson, out of the country at the time, was greatly satisfied by the scandal. In a letter to Gene Moskowitz, he wrote:

> It created something of a national scandal, which at least shows that one still has the capacity to draw blood! ... It really is extraordinary how the English bourgeoisie loses its discreet charm in a flash, the moment they are mocked or made to feel uneasy. And the artistic naïveté of the English is really boring: any departure from naturalism immediately finds itself labelled 'obscure', 'pretentious', 'under-graduate' or 'unnecessary'. It's like trying to read T. S. Eliot to an audience in a fish-and-chip shop.[3]

After screening *The Old Crowd* in what he called 'The New World' of Los Angeles, he walked out on development deals with three American studios to make *Britannia Hospital*, another film about Britain and Britishness. It completed the Mick Travis trilogy he had started with *if.....*

Appendix

An incomplete list of films seen theatrically by Lindsay Anderson between January 1965 and May 1967 before starting real work on the screenplay of *if*.... It is almost matched in number by live theatre productions he saw in Britain, Czechoslavakia and Poland in the same period. All quotes are taken from the draft document of my book, *Lindsay Anderson: The Diaries* (Methuen, 2004).

Abasheshey (India, Mrinal Sen) 'a human, poetic touch: but very slow'
Abschied von gestern (Germany, Alexander Kluge) 'I had to squeeze my
    hands tightly to prevent myself dozing off'
The Accused (Czech, Jan Kadar, Elmar Klos) 'bold, brilliantly compact'
The Affairs of Anatole (USA, Cecil B. de Mille) 'a drag honestly'
Akash Kusum (India, Sen)
Almost a Man (Italy, Vittorio De Seta)
And Miles to Go (India, S. Sukdev) – saw twice
Another Man's Face (Japan, Hiroshi Teshigahara) 'very powerful ... inter-
    esting abstracted style'
Answer to Violence (Poland, Jerzy Pasendorfer) 'not very remarkable'
Au hasard Balthazar (France, Robert Bresson)
Aunt Tula (Spain, Picazo)
The Battle for Algiers (Algeria, Gillo Pontecorvo) 'an impressive film, not
    great and epic, but quality'
Big City (Brazil, Carlos Diegues) 'not objectionable, but all over the place'
Black God, White Devil (Brazil, Glauber Rocha) 'hallucinatingly original
    and talented and too long!'
A Blonde in Love (Czech, Milos Forman) 'Full of superb and delicate poetic
    things: the reminiscence of Free Cinema is extraordinary'
The Boy Across the Street (Israel, Yosef Shalhin)
La Busca (Spain, Angelino Fons) 'some handsome photography, but the
    film cold'
Caprice (USA, Frank Tashlin) 'leaden'
The Ceiling (Czech, Vera Chytilova) 'free and unorthodox, bursting with
    film sense'

Changes in the Village (Sri Lanka, Lester James Piries) 'elegiac, near
Chekhovian grace'

Chappaqua (USA, Conrad Rooks) 'a brilliance of handling – particularly
Robert Franks's camera'

Charlie Bubbles (GB, Albert Finney)

Churulata (India, Satyajit Ray)

Courage Every Day (Czech, Evald Schorm) – three times: 'fine, moral
integrity of style'

Les Créatures (France, Agnes Varda) 'agonising'

The Crowd (USA, King Vidor) 'still a beautiful picture'

The Cry (Czech, Jaromil Jires) 'a tremendously talented first film'

Cuban documentaries (not known) 'splendid'

Cul de Sac (GB, Roman Polanski) 'dreadful'

La Curée (France, Roger Vadim)

Daisies (Czech, Vera Chytilova)

Dear John (Sweden, Lars Magnus Lindgren)

Diamonds of the Night (Czech, Jan Nemec)

The Drifter (USA – short – Alex Matter) 'rather charming'

Fahrenheit 451 (France/GB, François Truffaut)

Family of Man (Poland – short – Wladyslaw Slesicki) 'very accomplished'

Fanatic (GB, Silvio Narizzano) 'unpleasant but undeniably effective'

Fargo (USA, Brian Hutton) – twice – 'a good, sensitive, enjoyable picture'

First Day of Liberty (Poland, Aleksander Ford) 'impossibly old-fashioned
and melodramatic'

The First Teacher (Russia, Andrei Konchalovsky)

Four in the Morning (GB, Anthony Simmons) – three times: 'very impressed by its grim and brave integrity'

The Golden Rennet (Czech, Otakar Vavra) 'poetic'

The Goose Game (Spain, unknown) 'clever but shallow'

Grand Hotel (USA, Edmund Goulding)

Guns at Batsi (GB, John Guillermin) 'handled themes of colonialism and
independence with crassness and complacency'

Headmaster (India, Rabiuddin Ahmed)

Heroes of the Golden City (Turkey, unknown)

I was Happy Here (GB, Desmond Davis) 'really bad'

It Happened Here (GB, Kevin Brownlow) 'awfully good: fine atmosphere'

Joseph Kilian (Czech, Pavel Juracek, Jan Schmidt)

Jules et Jim (France, François Truffaut) – twice: 'once more I am aston-
ished at the flair and originality of the shooting and editing'

Kampala (India, Uday Shakar)

Kanchenjunga (India, Satyajit Ray) 'charming, well constructed pic'

The Knack (GB, Richard Lester)

Konkurs (Czech, Milos Forman) 'most poetic, original and sensitive'

Kwaidan (Japan, Masaki Kobayashi)

Life at the Top (GB, Ted Kotcheff) 'really awful'

The Logic Game (GB, Philip Saville) 'loathed'

Lord Jim (GB, Richard Brooks) 'silly, shallow ... poor, disjointed performance by Peter O'Toole'

The Lost Years (Czech, Otakar Vavra)

The Luck of Ginger Coffey (USA, Irvin Kershner)

Mahanagar (India, Satyajit Ray)

Man at the Bottom (Czech, unknown) 'pedestrian in some of its handling:
yet remarkable for content'

Le Mistral (Netherlands, Joris Ivens) 'brilliant, purposeless camera'

Moment of Truth (Italy, Francesco Rosi)

Morgan (GB, Karel Reisz) 'nothing is organic: it is all painfully thought
out, rationalised, no humour'

My Best Wish (Czech documentary)

Nattlek (Sweden, Mai Zetterling) 'simple, sentimental Freudianism ...
awful'

Nobody Waved Goodbye (Canada, Don Owen)

On the River Bank (India, Tyaro Nadir Parey) 'a pretentious and I'm afraid
quite untalented piece'

One Way Pendulum (GB, Peter Yates) 'competent'

The Organiser (Italy, Mario Monicelli) 'lacking real depth: but impressive
in bits'

Our Dancing Daughters (USA, Harry Beaumont) 'tedious, old-fashioned,
moralistic'

Pearls of the Deep (Czech, various) – three times: 'struck again by the brilliance of the camerawork'

Peter and Pavla (Czech, Milos Forman) 'excellent and charming'

Play (GB, Samuel Beckett) 'storm of whistling, booing and slow hand
clapping – which gave a certain avant-garde dignity to the occasion!'

Postmaster (India, Satyajit Ray)

Privilege (GB, Peter Watkins) 'sad ... can Britain not produce a new,
thirty-one-year old director who is not an adolescent?'

Raven's End (Swedish, Bo Widerberg) 'austere, melancholic and poetic'

Red and Blue (GB, Tony Richardson) 'Tony's usual virtuosity ... and a
phoney, masturbatory sensuality'

The Red Desert (Italy, Michelangelo Antonioni) 'boring: i.e. visually
monotonous ... characters psychologically underdeveloped'

Repulsion (Poland/GB, Roman Polanski) 'clever but rather thin, really quite boring'

Ride of the Valkyries (GB, Peter Brook) 'I could rejoice I suppose at the utterly disastrous amateurism of this'

The Saragossa Manuscript (Poland, Wojciech Has)

Shakuntala (India, Shantaram) 'splendid sequences of the heroine subduing a posse of ravening lions by her yogi-detachment.'

Shenandoah (USA, Andrew V. McLaglen) 'good period, bad acting'

A Shop on the Square (Czech, Jan Kadar and Elmar Klos) – three times

La Soldadera (Mexico, Jose Bolanos) 'doesn't convince as the work of a director'

Stranded (USA, Juleen Compton) 'rather sympathetic, naïf and (I think) promising'

Thérèse Desqueyroux (France, Georges Franju)

The Train (USA, John Frankenheimer) 'a dull "made" picture with no real tension'

Walkover (Poland, Jerzy Skolimowsky) – twice: 'brilliant, allusive, a bit limited perhaps, but very clever'

The Way Things are (Yugoslavia, Vladan Slijepeevic)

The War Game (GB, Peter Watkins)

The Wild Angels (USA, Roger Corman) 'shallow, melodramatic, certainly vital but preposterous'

Wuthering Heights (India, Ashok Kumar)

Young Cassidy (GB, Jack Cardiff) 'I should have done it'

The Young Nun (Italy, Bruno Paolinelli) 'a work of great elegance and subtlety'

Notes

1. THE CONTEXT

1 *St Ronan's News*, Easter 1935; copy in the Lindsay Anderson Collection, Stirling University (hereafter Anderson-Stirling).

2 Copy in Anderson-Stirling.

3 Sutton, *Lindsay Anderson: The Diaries*, p. 28 (hereafter *Anderson Diaries*). All diary quotes are taken from the working draft of my book. Page numbers refer to their place in the first published edition.

4 *Anderson Diaries*, pp. 38–9.

5 Ibid., pp. 31–2.

6 Ibid,. pp. 32–3.

7 Ibid., p. 47.

8 Anderson, 'Angles of Approach', pp. 5–8.

9 'Free Cinema' programme (1956), p. 1.

10 Allison Graham is the author of the excellent book *Lindsay Anderson*.

11 Letter from Lindsay Anderson to Tony Richardson, copy in Anderson-Stirling.

12 Conversation with the author, 4 September 2002.

13 Conversation with the author, 14 October 2002.

14 *Anderson Diaries*, pp. 45–6.

15 *if....* 1968 pressbook, p. 56.

16 *Anderson Diaries*, pp. 75–6.

17 Anderson, 'Homage to Cannes', 7 March 1987, from the manuscript in Anderson-Stirling.

18 'Il Cinema di Poesia', reprinted in Pier Paolo Pasolini, *Heretical Empiricism* (Indiana University Press, 1988).

19 *Anderson Diaries*, p. 98

20 *Anderson Diaries*, previously unpublished entry.

21 Ibid., 7 February 1965.

22 *Anderson Diaries*, pp. 107–8.

23 *if....* pressbook, p. 15.

24 *The Times*, 19 May 1965, p. 39.

25 *Anderson Diaries*, p. 116.

26 Ibid,. p. 139.

27 *Anderson Diaries*, p. 51.

28 *Anderson Diaries*, previously unpublished entry.

29 A copy is in Anderson-Stirling.

30 *Anderson Diaries*, pp. 169–73.

31 Ibid., pp. 130–1.

32 Anderson-Stirling.

33 *Anderson Diaries*, p. 183.

34 *if....* pressbook, p. 47.

35 Ibid., p. 55.

36 Ibid., p. 58.

37 Ibid.

38 Conversation with the author, 12 July 2004.

39 Conversation with the author, 10 July 2004.

40 *if....* pressbook, p. 37.

41 Conversation with the author, 10 July 2004.

42 Malcolm McDowell, 'Lindsay Anderson: A Personal Remembrance', Edinburgh, 23 August 2004, (hereafter McDowell Remembrance Talk).

43 Askwith, *The Confessions of Robin Askwith*, pp. 186–7.

44 Conversation with the author, 11 July 2003.

45 Conversation with the author, 12 August 2004.

46 Adam Mills, *The Cheltonion*, 1968, pp. 6–8.

47 Gladwell, 'Editing Anderson's *if....* ', pp. 24–33.

48 Conversation with the author, 11 July 2003.

49 Conversation with the author, 25 May 2002.

50 *if....* pressbook, p. 39.

51 Askwith, *The Confessions of Robin Askwith*, pp. 192–3.

52 Conversation with the author, 4 September 2002.

53 Ashcroft, '"IF" Twenty-five Years on', pp. 6–8.

53 Sherwin, *Going Mad in Hollywood*, pp. 22–3.

2. THE NARRATIVE

1 *Anderson Diaries*, pp. 193–99.

2 Anderson, 'Two Inches off the Ground', pp. 131–3, 160.

3 *Observer*, 21 March 1965, p. 24.

4 Anderson, 'Notes for a Preface', p. 10.

5 *Anderson Diaries*, p. 51.

6 Ibid., p. 143.

7 Conversation with the author, 11 July 2003.

8 McDowell Remembrance Talk.

9 Ibid.

10 'Too Stark for Mr Chips', *Sunday Telegraph*, 15 December 1968.

11 Conversation with the author, 25 May 2002.

12 Ibid.

13 Anderson, 'Get Out and Push', pp. 155–6.

14 *Anderson Diaries*, p. 33.

15 Conversation with the author, 12 August 2004. Gladwell also mentions the scene in 'Editing Anderson's *if....*'.

16 *If – the Shooting Script*, Anderson and Sherwin.

17 Ibid.

18 *If – the Headmaster's Script*; also included in the novelisation by David Sherwin (Sphere, 1969).

3. THE RECEPTION

1 Letter from John Trevelyan to Lindsay Anderson, 1 July 1968 (Anderson-Stirling).

2 Letter from John Trevelyan to Lindsay Anderson, 27 August 1968 (Anderson-Stirling).

3 Document in the Anderson archive at Stirling. The film was censored on 30 April 1969.

4 Letter from Terence Feely (Paramount UK) to Lindsay Anderson (Anderson-Stirling).

5 Ashcroft, 'Lindsay Conned Us All', p. 1.

6 Anderson-Stirling. The collection of clippings is undated.

7 Letter from Paul Griffin to Lindsay Anderson, 17 January 1969 (Anderson-Stirling).

8 *Anderson Diaries*, pp. 194–5.

9 Anderson, interview in *Pangolin* (February 1970).

10 Derek Malcolm, 'Sight and Sound-off', *Guardian*, December 1968.

11 Penelope Mortimer, 'Anderson's Masterwork', *Observer*, 22 December 1968, p. 19.

12 Dilys Powell, 'Much Virtue in If', *Sunday Times*, 22 December 1968, p. 24.

13 Patrick Gibbs, 'Public School Parody', *Telegraph*, 20 December 1968.

14 John Coleman, 'Mr Anderson's Anarchy', *New Statesman*, 20 December 1968.

15 David Wilson, *Monthly Film Bulletin*, February 1969, pp. 25–6.

16 Joseph Gelmis, '*If* is a Masterpiece that May Offend', undated article (Anderson-Stirling).

17 Richard Schickel, 'Angry Knot in the Old School Tie', *Life*, 66 (28 February), p. 8.

18 Robert Kotlowitz, 'Aspects of Love', *Harper's* magazine, April 1969 pp. 115–6.

19 Albert Johnson, *Film Quarterly*, pp. 48–52.

20 Conversation with the author, 11 July 2003.

21 All figures are from documents in Anderson-Stirling.

22 Conversation with the author, 25 May 2002.

23 *If(2)....* first draft screenplay by David Sherwin and Lindsay Anderson.

CONCLUSION

1 *Anderson Diaries*, pp. 491–2.

2 If one doesn't include the filmed stage productions *In Celebration* (1974) and *Look Back in Anger* (1980).

3 Letter from Lindsay Anderson to Gene Moskowitz, 23 February 1979.

Sources

Anderson, Lindsay,'Angles of Approach', *Sequence* (Winter, 1947).

— 'Get Out and Push', Declaration (1957).

— 'Homage to Cannes' (1987).

— 'Notes for a Preface', *if....* a film by Lindsay Anderson and David Sherwin (Plexus, London, 1969).

— 'Two Inches off the Ground' *Sight and Sound* (Winter, 1957).

Ashcroft, David, 'Lindsay Conned Us All' *Coll*, 14 December 1968, p. 1. (vol. 5, no. 4).

— '*if....* Twenty-five Years on', *HMC Journal*, 1994.

Askwith, Robin, *The Confessions of Robin Askwith* (Ebury Press, 1999).

Cohen, Jules, 'Interview with Lindsay Anderson', *Pangolin*, vol. 1, no. 1 (February 1970).

Gladwell, David, 'Editing Anderson's *if....* ', *Screen*, vol. 10, no. 1 (January/February 1969).

Graham, Allison, *Lindsay Anderson* (Twayne Publishers, 1981).

Hedling, Erik, *Lindsay Anderson, Maverick Film-Maker* (Cassell, 1998).

if.... 1968 pressbook (Memorial Productions).

Kalton, Graham, *The Public Schools: A Factual Survey* (Longmans, 1966).

Public Schools Commission. First Report, vol. 1 (Her Majesty's Stationery Office, 1968).

Sherwin, David, *if....* novelisation (Sphere, 1969).

— *Going Mad in Hollywood* (Andre Deutsch, 1996).

Sutton, Paul (ed.), *Lindsay Anderson: The Diaries* (Methuen, 2004).

Sussex, Elizabeth, *Lindsay Anderson* (Praeger, 1969).

NEWSPAPERS AND MAGAZINES

The Cheltonion; *Film Quarterly*; *Guardian*; *Harper's*; *Life*; *Monthly Film Bulletin*; *New Statesman*; *Observer*; *Sunday Telegraph*; *Sunday Times*; *Telegraph*; *The Times*

INTERVIEWS

Graham Crowden, 14 October 2002

Jocelyn Herbert, 4 September 2002

Malcolm McDowell, 25 May 2002 and 10 July 2004
Brian Pettifer, 12 August 2004
Rupert Webster, 11 July 2003

UNPUBLISHED MATERIAL

Lindsay Anderson Diaries – material excluded from the published edition.
— 'An Untitled Screenplay' (1942).
'Crusaders' – screenplay by David Sherwin and John Howlett.
if.... Headmaster's Script by David Sherwin.
if.... Shooting Script by Lindsay Anderson and David Sherwin.
if(2).... first draft screenplay by David Sherwin and Lindsay Anderson.
Call-sheet for Brian Pettifer.
Letter from Alan Bennett, undated.
Letter from John Betjeman, 10 September 1969.
Letter from John Boorman, undated.
Letter from Sean Bury, undated.
Letter from David Cornwell (John Le Carré), 15 May 1969.
Letter from Michael Croft, 19 December 1969.
Letter from Richard Everett, 6 December 1968.
Letter from Terence Feely, 6 September 1968.
Letter from James Fox, undated.
Letter from Paul Griffin, 17 January 1969.
Letter from Rex Harrison, undated.
Letter from Akira Kurosawa, 16 June 1969.
Letter from Richard Lester, 23 December 1968.
Letter from Bernard Miles, undated.
Letter from Brian Pettifer, undated.
Letter from Harold Pinter, 15 January 1969.
Letter from Vanessa Redgrave, undated.
Letter from Guy Ross, undated.
Letter from Robert Swann, undated.
Letter from Hugh Thomas, 11 January 1969.
Letter from John Trevelyan, 1st July 1968.
Letter from John Trevelyan, 27 August 1968.
Letter to Jack Landman, 1976
Letter to Gene Moskowitz, 23 February 1979.
Letter to Tony Richardson, 17 October 1985
St Ronan's News, Easter 1935.